Faithful to the Call

Women in Ministry

Carla D. Sunberg, Editor

THE FOUNDRY
PUBLISHING®

Copyright © 2022 by The Foundry Publishing®

The Foundry Publishing
PO Box 419527
Kansas City, MO 64141
thefoundrypublishing.com

978-0-8341-4102-5

Printed in the
United States of America

Cover designer: Merit Kathan
Interior designer: Sharon Page

Library of Congress Cataloging-in-Publication Data
Names: Sunberg, Carla D., editor.
Title: Faithful to the call: women in ministry / Carla D. Sunberg, editor.
Description: Kansas City, MO : The Foundry Publishing, [2022] | Includes bibliographical ref-erences. | Summary: "In Faithful to the Call, scholars, pastors, and ministry leaders make the Wesleyan case for women in ministry. They offer historical, biblical, theological, and practical evidence for why women should be faithful to the call when God gifts and invites them to participate in God's grand story"— Provided by publisher.
Identifiers: LCCN 2021046176 (print) | LCCN 2021046177 (ebook) | ISBN 9780834141025 | ISBN 9780834141032 (ebook)
Subjects: LCSH: Women clergy. | Women in church work. | Church of the Nazarene—Doctrines.
Classification: LCC BV676 .F35 2022 (print) | LCC BV676 (ebook) | DDC 262.14082—dc23
LC record available at https://lccn.loc.gov/2021046176
LC ebook record available at https://lccn.loc.gov/2021046177

10 9 8 7 6 5 4 3 2 1

Be not disobedient to the heavenly calling.
—John Wesley

Contents

Foreword

The Church of the Nazarene, from the very moment of its entry into the denominational world in 1894, settled the matter that women are to be ordained for ministry and are suitable for all opportunities to which God has chosen and called them. This affirmation derives from the character of God and from Scripture, where we find that God's creation has been set free from the curse of the fall.

Women, called by God to ministry, do not answer the call because a man refused or because God could not find someone else—but because God chose, gifted, and ordained creation of both male and female humans to this heavenly calling to proclaim the gospel. This gift of calling was delegated to the church on the day of Pentecost with equality and without prejudice.

The women who are obedient to the call are commended for the strategic and significant place they have historically filled and continue to fill in the life and ministry of the church.

I commend these qualified writers who share their heart and talents with us. Enjoy the read as you answer a heavenly calling.

Rev. Dr. Nina Gunter
General Superintendent Emerita
Church of the Nazarene

Introduction

On that first Easter morning, the women went to the tomb to prepare Jesus's body, but they soon discovered that he was not there—he had risen. They departed from that place on a mission, for they had been told to go and share the good news, to evangelize, to let others know that Jesus had risen from the dead. God trusted the female followers of Jesus Christ to be the very first to tell others the transformational news of the resurrection. Jesus empowered his female disciples to participate in his mission to go and make disciples. Today, women make up more than half of those who attend church, and they are pillars of congregations around the globe.

Although women make up more than half the church, there are still those who are uncomfortable with women in church leadership, and as a result there have been seasons when the ministry of women has been under threat. As part of the Wesleyan-Holiness tradition, women clergy have been part of the Church of the Nazarene from the founding days of the denomination. This book is an effort to bring together our history and theology in a way that helps us understand why God would want to use women in service in the church, just like on that first resurrection day. Time and again, it seems we need to revisit God's promise of restoration and the way in which the restored image of God is revealed through the use of women in the kingdom of God. The image of God restored in humanity remains at the very heart of the holiness message.

Historically, there have been those who have focused on particular texts from the New Testament that can be a challenge. What have been missed, however, are the passages that tell of the ways Jesus and his apostles partnered and served with women in ministry. Some of the very first disciples who were obedient to the call of Jesus were women. If we follow Jesus on the journey from Galilee to the cross, and eventually the garden tomb, we see that the inner circle of followers included a group of women who refused to abandon him. Once Jesus called, they faithfully followed.

Today, God is raising up a new generation of women who are answering the call and leaning into a myriad of opportunities for ministry. As the church's ministry expands throughout the world, we find women who are partnering with their male counterparts in fulfilling the Great Commission. The resultant synergy can be witnessed in the fruitfulness of their labors. The church is healthy when God's sons and daughters are united together in the work of God—but the opposite is also true. When those partnerships are broken or strained, the church itself suffers. That's where the champions step in, becoming voices in the spaces where women have none. It requires the entire church community to embrace God's calling upon sons *and* daughters.

Meet the Lioness

On the continent of Africa, we find a woman who answered the call of God in her life. This woman, Rev. Bessie Luisa Timoteo Mucavele Chambo (or Tsambe)[1], is known as the "Lioness of

---

1. Dr. Filimão Chambo is the 42nd general superintendent in the Church of the Nazarene. This is the story of his mother, Bessie, and her call to ministry. The family name in their native language is Tsambe, or Ntsembe, but it was changed to Chambo by the colonial Portuguese leadership of Mozambique.

Africa" because, from the moment she knew she was to be a minister, she never allowed circumstance to get in the way of obedience. Eventually she pastored the Maputo Central Church of the Nazarene in Mozambique. Under her leadership, the church grew to nearly three thousand members and planted more than twenty new congregations. She was also a wife who partnered in her husband's ministry and invested in her children. Today one of her sons, Dr. Filimão Chambo, serves as a general superintendent in the Church of the Nazarene.

Bessie's story begins quite humbly. The daughter of a Nazarene pastor and his wife in Jatigue, Manjacaze, in Mozambique, she was born in the Nazarene Mission Hospital in Machulane (Tavane) in the province of Gaza. Her father, Rev. Timoteo Mucavele, and his wife, Rosta Zandamela Mucavele, were faithful servants of God who dedicated their lives not only to teaching but also to showing their children the way of truth. This way of life included participation in household chores, but there was also plenty of time for play. At the age of five, Bessie's playtime with her siblings was mostly spent singing and praising God, followed by a time of preaching—and, normally, Bessie was the preacher. Worldly songs were not permitted.

When she was a teenager, the family moved to the city of Xai-Xai, where they pastored but also had responsibility for the neighboring wheat fields. Bessie accepted Jesus as her Savior at a revival meeting for children in Tavane in June of 1958. In Xai-Xai, the children had the noble task of scaring the birds away from the wheat in the fields. During the workday, Bessie routinely gathered the other young people for a devotional time; they sang together, then Bessie preached and led them in prayer. God's hand was on her throughout her childhood and in her Christian growth. In her teen years she took great pleasure in helping out at church—whether leading music, teaching Sunday school, or serving as the Sunday school secretary. She enjoyed all these things but never considered becoming a pastor. At one point her father tried to enroll her in Bible school, but she told him she didn't want to be a pastor. She simply wanted to be a true model of a Christian and continue to serve God in the ways she had already been serving.

Bessie was well educated through the local and parochial school systems, and attended her first two years of high school at the technical institute in Joao Belo. She then went to the commercial school in Lourenço Marques (known as the capital city of Maputo today) to study business and economics. Her studies were interrupted, and she returned to Tavane to teach. Throughout this entire time, she was supported by her parents, her older sister, and a missionary named Bessie Tallackson, who helped subsidize her education.

On the night of November 6, 1966, during family prayer, her father read a passage that spoke of a divine calling. Her dad preached, they prayed together, and then the family went to bed. Bessie couldn't sleep, so she went outside to pray. Her intention was to study hard and make money to help her parents—never to marry a pastor, or the son of a pastor, much less *become* one herself! All she knew was that the pastors around her were poor, without much chance of economic improvement. But that night, she responded yes to the divine call, thanks to the prayers of her parents and the believers around the world who prayed that God would call more workers into the great harvest.

Bessie met her husband, Manuel Filimão Chambo, at the Nazarene Mission in Machulane, where they both served as teachers. He was a member of Maputo Central Church, a Portuguese congregation. The missionaries asked him to be the fourth-grade teacher. That year Bessie also became a member of Maputo Central Church, and the missionaries asked her to teach in the same mission. When she met her husband, neither planned to enter the pastoral ministry. They thought they would serve the Lord by teaching, but God had other plans for both of them, and Manuel started pastoring in 1968. They married the following year.

Bessie's ministry became focused on her growing family. She and her husband were fully committed to the spiritual development of their children. They invested in Bible adventure books that taught spiritual growth. They taught their children to sing evangelical choruses, to read and understand the Word of God, to memorize Scripture, and to pray. As the children grew, in addition to the time designated for chores around the house and schoolwork, they also spent time together reading spiritual books and, of course, the Bible. Bessie and her husband helped the children read through the Bible from January to December each year. Every member of the family had to take their turn as the preacher during the family devotional service. They participated in all the church activities—Sunday school and discipleship, worship services, Caravan, Vacation Bible School, and programs for children and youth. While raising her children, Bessie went back to school, studying at the Nazarene Bible Institute in Maputo, today called Seminário Nazareno em Moçambique.

Her husband, known by his traditional name, Rev. Ntshambe, went on to become the district superintendent for the Church of the Nazarene of Maputo, Matola, and Boane. On Sundays they regularly traveled together to visit the churches. Sunday, April 9, 1989, became a catalyst to fulfilling the will of God in Bessie's life. They visited the church in Boane, but because they hadn't announced their visit, they were surprised to arrive and discover that the pastor was absent. They learned from church members that the pastor had officially retired from his secular job, and wasn't taking care of his church flock.

The following two Sundays, they attended other churches in the district, but on April 29, Bessie couldn't sleep. Thoughts of the situation in Boane tortured her all night, so before their morning prayer time, she proposed a possible solution to her husband: she would go to Boane to support the church until the district could send a new pastor. Her husband agreed, and they prayed together. After this they began their family devotional time, and then her husband told the family that Bessie would go the very next Sunday to take on the flock in Boane on a temporary basis. Their fourth son, Noah, was assigned to accompany his mother on this mission. On August 9, 1991, after she had been unofficially pastoring the church in Boane for more than two years, Bessie Luisa Timoteo Mucavele Chambo (Tsambe) was ordained as an elder in the Church of the Nazarene while attending the Africa Regional Conference in South Africa.

The district asked her to care for the church until November 1991. Shortly before she completed her service in Boane, she received a letter asking her to pastor Maputo Central Church. At the time, she asked her husband what he thought of her accepting the appointment because she had planned to return to partner with her husband in his responsibilities on the district. He suggested that she pray and ask the One who had called her to guide her. She thanked him and sought the will of God. The result was that, on November 3, 1991, she said farewell to the Boane church and, on November 10, 1991, took charge of Maputo Central Church, where she pastored until June 6, 2013.

Along the way, Bessie had champions in her life. Her parents, a missionary, her husband, and her previous district superintendent all saw something in her, and encouraged her to follow God's call. Beyond responding to the call, these people intentionally helped her get the training and education she would need, buying her books and resources. Her husband encouraged her to go to seminars and workshops, and he prayed for her. Bessie said, "All of these factors together contributed positively for the continued growth of my ministerial development and, above all, for my spiritual growth. I can affirm that I am who I am thanks to the support of my husband."

The Lioness of Africa was obedient to the call of God on her life. Not only did she respond to the formal call to ministry, but her own life was also a living testimony to the work of Jesus in the world. She poured herself into her children, and they fell in love with Jesus too. Bessie would tell us that we are to "influence believers in a positive way, entrust them with tasks to encourage them to discover their spiritual gifts, and train workers for the advancement of the work of God. Never try to do everything alone!" Finally, she advises women who are called to "have attentive ears to listen and eyes fixed on the One who calls. He will never leave you. For God, there are not men, nor women, but only 'servants of God.'"[2]

Rev. Dr. Carla D. Sunberg
General Superintendent
Church of the Nazarene

---

2. All direct quotations attributed to Rev. Bessie Chambo are from a personal interview with her that took place in August 2020.

One
The Historical Presence of Women in the Church

Rev. Dr. Diane Leclerc
Minister and Professor
United States

Nazarene women clergy represent a long history of women preachers in the tradition known as the Wesleyan-Holiness Movement. Methodist women preached shortly after Methodism was born. Holiness women preached *when* the Holiness Movement was born. And Wesleyan-Holiness women have preached ever since. This fact is often overlooked by broader Christian historians and ecclesiastical analysts, who mistakenly see women preachers and female ordination as a later-twentieth-century phenomenon that rode the second wave of feminism that began in the 1960s.

The Holiness Movement, however, occurred squarely in the middle of the *first* wave of feminism in the nineteenth century. The first wave of feminism was socially vocal and active on issues of equality such as slavery and abolition, the rights of non-whites and immigrants, the rights of the poor, and the rights of women—known outside the church as suffrage and recognized inside the church as the right to hold every position of leadership, including ordination. Nearly all of the denominations that arose from the Holiness Movement affirmed the full equality of women from their inception, including the Church of the Nazarene. Such views on equality came from holiness theology itself, arising out of the account of Pentecost as central to the movement's identity.

It is unfortunate that so many people now associated with these denominations do not know this history, or have lost the Wesleyan-Holiness theology on which human equality is founded. As a result, women have recently found it necessary to defend their right to preach, even in denominations that have *never* questioned or debated such a right. It is perhaps wise to ask, and answer, whether Wesley's ideas about women preaching appeared out of the blue, or whether there is historical support for women's leadership in the church. This chapter will briefly review the history of women in the early church and the medieval period before turning to a longer discussion of women in Methodism and in Holiness churches.

The Early Church

There is some historical evidence that women were, in fact, priests in the first century and after, due to the fact that churches were hosted in homes—or, in other words, the women's main sphere of cultural influence. It wasn't until the church became more of a public entity (advocated by the Patristic Father Tertullian) that women were no longer seen as legitimate leaders in the church. This does not mean they were not still powerful and influential. We begin with a discussion of two areas of such empowerment after the time of the New Testament—martyrdom and asceticism.

In Christianity's earliest days, Christians were seen as a Jewish sect, and thus were afforded the same religious protections given to the Jews at the time. But as Christianity became more and more distinct from the Jewish faith because of masses of gentile converts, and because of the development of their own set of sacred writings, these protections no longer applied in the minds of the authorities. As a result, when Christians did not worship the emperor or the pagan gods, they were brutally persecuted and martyred.

In the second century, the persecution of Christians was often sporadic and regional. Some of the most famous of these were the persecutions and martyrdoms in Lyons and Vienna in 177, and in North Africa in 202 and after, where men and women were killed. These persecutions are recorded for us as savage and horrific. When Decius became Emperor in 249, the local persecutions became empire-wide. But the worst persecution was still to come. In 303 Diocletian came to power. His rage against the Christians was even more aggressive than that of his predecessors.

Men and women died for their faith in equal numbers. When it came to persecution, gender was not a factor. In fact, interestingly, women were even more exalted than men in the portrayals. Something intriguing happens in these accounts. In light of the stratification of Roman society, the very highest and most admired martyrs of Christ were actually the very lowest in the eyes of the world. The highest and most admired martyrs were women—more than that, they were slave women. A man's martyrdom was seen as noble. But a man might be able to endure the brutality of martyrdom because of his own physical strength. So the weaker the person was, the more commendable the martyrdom—because, the weaker the person, the more they were seen as empowered by God alone, and the more trust in the Holy Spirit they displayed. A slave woman, then, could only have endured because of Christ's power at work within her and, thus, was the best witness.

One of the most important accounts of any martyrdom recorded was the account of Perpetua and her slave, Felicitas. They were highly revered heroines of the early church. Central to the original martyrdom account is Perpetua's relationship with her family. She had an infant son with her in prison while she awaited death. Similarly, Felicitas was about to give birth. Perpetua's pagan father tried, unsuccessfully, to convince her to deny her faith so she could raise her child. She refused his pleas, and he had the child taken from her. Felicitas gave birth. The account records the witness of their deaths in an intriguing way: God freed them of their earthly (even motherly) responsibilities so they could fulfill their calling as witnesses. Only then were they both sent to the Arena to die. They died displaying incredible bravery as they testified loudly to the God they served.

Interestingly, the early church also shows ascetic women to be uniquely empowered. The ascetic movement can be found early in Christianity but became more significant after Constantine declared Christianity legal. Masses of persons from the Roman populace were baptized as Christians immediately. Certainly this "watered down" the faith. The question quickly arose: how are we to perceive who is truly devoted and holy now? No longer were there martyrs to hold the highest place of holy honor. It is no coincidence that, just after Constantine's edict of toleration, a new martyrdom developed. And women were right in the middle of it.

This new martyrdom was the rise of asceticism. If one no longer had the opportunity to be literally crucified with Christ, there was at least the option of metaphorical crucifixion, or self-mortification. Persons began to practice rigorous spiritual disciplines as a means of spiritual purification. This further developed into the practice of hermitages. Men, and a few women, headed for the Egyptian desert in particular, where they lived primarily in solitude, with few interactions with one another. These, from then on, were known as the Desert Fathers and Mothers. Eventually these hermits formed communities that gave rise to what we know today as monasteries or convents. In either case, the ascetics were identified by other Christians as the new holy ones who replaced the martyrs as Christian heroes.

During this time, female ascetics were afforded freedoms unavailable to married women. They were able to travel freely, they were educated at a higher level, even sometimes to the point of teaching men, and they were praised for their virtues. We have the writings of male ascetics who praise women strongly, counting them as equals. Women such as Paula, Marcella, Olympia, Melania the Elder, and Melania the Younger are only a few of a vast number of women who followed in this way. Of particular note is Macrina, the sister of Gregory of Nyssa and Basil. Both of these church fathers attribute their training in spirituality to this remarkable woman. She is seen as one of the great saints of the church. The early church period of history shows that women were active and revered, and often seen as equal to men in their faith and contributions to God's kingdom.

The Medieval Period

The medieval period was a time of great diversity among people, particularly between the rich and the poor. Women who were commoners often lived difficult lives. But, in a similar way to the early church period, ascetic women were given more freedom. We find during this period very influential women among those who were nuns and/or mystics, including: Hildegard of Bingen (1098–1179); Gertrude the Great (1256–1302); Mechtilde (1217–1282); Julian of Norwich (1342–1416); Catherine of Siena (1347–80); and, moving into the era of the Protestant Reformation, Teresa of Avila (1515–82). These women were writers, theologians, and even ecclesiastical leaders who influenced popes and kings. We will elaborate on the last three.

Catherine of Siena (1347–80) was known for her positive influence on the politics of the Catholic Church. After years of solitude, she decided to leave her cell and engage the world for Christ. She had the ear of the pope. She is also especially known for her theology, two aspects of which we will name here. First, Catherine seemed to have an intuitive grasp of truth that she attributed to the Holy Spirit. She believed that the Spirit alone led women and men into "the depths of God." "When this happens the person so graced has a knowledge of God which, while in harmony with the knowledge arrived at by one's faith-enlightened intellect, is deeper and more perfect."[1] Secondly and similarly, Catherine demonstrated the fact that the essential characteristic of mysticism is its affective dimension. Catherine described this affectual awareness as an ability "to taste and see the depths of the Trinity."[2] Like Catherine, John Wesley will later have a strong place in his theology for this affectual dimension of Christian truth and faith.

Julian of Norwich (1342–1416) was an English mystic. She was an anchoress at the Church of Saint Julian in Norwich. We do not actually know her real name. Through a series of visions, Julian developed an intense belief in God as loving, compassionate, and merciful. Her work, *Sixteen Revelations of*

---

1. Mary O'Driscoll, "Catherine the Theologian," *Spirituality Today* Vol. 40, No. 1 (Spring 1988), http://www.domcentral.org/library/spir-2day/884011odriscoll.html.

2. Catherine of Siena, *Dialogue*, trans. Suzanne Nofke (New York: Paulist Press, 1980). See chapters 61, 167.

Divine Love, is said to anticipate some of Martin Luther's theology of grace. Although she lived with great physical pain, Julian's theology was optimistic. She spoke of God's love in terms of joy as opposed to law and duty. For Julian, suffering was not punishment from God. She believed that God loved everyone and would offer grace to any in need. Like Catherine of Siena, Julian's theology was unusually holistic. They both avoided a body-soul dualism that was common in other mystics of their day. Julian's theology, like Wesley's, was absolutely centered on God's love.

Teresa of Avila (1515–82) was born of nobility in Spain. She made the decision to become a Carmelite nun after a series of family losses and her own ill health. Teresa is known as a mystic, theologian, church reformer, and particularly for her instructions on prayer. In light of Carmelite laxity at the time, she joined with Saint John of the Cross, and separated into a new order known as Discalced Carmelites, which received papal approval in 1580. Her mystical writings on prayer—*The Interior Castle* and *The Way of Perfection*—have been influential to the present day. The metaphors offered in these writings have been used in holiness contexts as helps for understanding entire devotion and sanctification.

The influence of women such as these shows that the empowerment of women continued from the early church all the way to the days of John Wesley.

Women in Early Methodism

Methodism in the second half of the eighteenth century, under the leadership of John Wesley, reveals a growing acceptance of the giftedness of the women of the movement. This giftedness included the leadership of bands and societies, pastoral care of the sick and dying, public prayer and testimony, and eventually preaching, due to the recognition by Wesley of the call of many extraordinary women. John Wesley was influenced by women throughout his life—beginning, of course, with his mother, Susanna.

Susanna was a strong figure in John Wesley's spiritual development, but she also modeled leadership in the larger ecclesial setting. Having had his mother model women's potential for spiritual leadership, he made it an early part of his own pastoral practice. After beginning the revival in England, Wesley discovered that a high percentage of the members of the societies were women. He quickly allowed women to lead bands, and then societies, even when men were members. In the setting of the societies, women were encouraged to pray publicly, offer personal testimony, and exhort the other members, often using Scripture as their basis.

Numerous women across England made steps toward public preaching. Wesley offered an overtly positive response to women assuming ministerial roles. From his sermon "On Visiting the Sick," he preached these bold words:

Herein there is no difference; "there is neither male nor female in Christ Jesus." Indeed it has long passed for the maxim with many that "women are only to be seen, not heard." And accordingly many of them are brought up in such a manner as if they were only designed for agreeable playthings! But is this doing honour to the sex? or is it a real kindness to them? No; it is the deepest unkindness; it is horrid cruelty; it is mere Turkish barbarity. And I know not how any woman of sense and spirit can submit to it. Let all you that have it in your power assert the right which God of nature has given you. Yield not to that vile bondage any longer! You, as well as men, are rational creatures. You, like them, were made in the image of God; you are equally

candidates for immortality; you too are called of God. . . .
Be "not disobedient to the heavenly calling."[3]

Sarah Crosby, considered to be the first of the women
preachers of early Methodism, experienced glimpses of true
equality as she exercised her gifts with ever-increasing freedom
and approval by Wesley. Sarah (also called Sally) Crosby was
born November 7, 1729, in Leeds. She was made a class leader
in 1751; although she felt inadequate for the task, she was effective as a leader, devoting much of her time to the society. In
1757, she professed an experience of entire sanctification that
became central to her ministry and her preaching throughout
her life. She also experienced another vivid incident that she
recorded in a letter to Wesley:

> Not long after this as I was praying, my soul was overwhelmed
> with the power of God; I seemed to see the Lord Jesus be-
> fore me, and said, "Lord, I am ready to follow thee, not only
> to prison, but to death, if thou wilt give me strength;" and he
> spake these words to my heart, "feed my sheep."[4]

That calling would never leave her, and would expand in
meaning through the years. By 1771 Wesley seemed to move
beyond the pragmatic benefit of women preachers and began
to wrestle with the idea theologically as he reflected on the
whole nature of the Methodist movement. During this decade,
Sarah Crosby became an itinerant preacher, at times traveling
with Wesley himself. "Sarah Crosby's reputation as a remark-

---

3. John Wesley, "On Visiting the Sick" in *The Works of John Wesley*,
Thomas Jackson, 3rd ed. (Grand Rapids: Baker Books, 2005), 7:125–26.
4. Quoted in Zachariah Taft, *Biographical Sketches of the Lives and Public Ministry of Various Holy Women* vol. 1 (Nashville: Methodist Publishing
House, 1992), 36.

able preacher soon preceded her wherever she went [as did] her indefatigable public labors."[5]

We see a development in Wesley's thought. While ideals of equality were in place early in his life, his relationship with these women would force him to hone his ideology with ever-increasing clarity. Early in his career, he interpreted the difficult passages of Scripture concerning women rather rigidly. But through his experiences with women such as Sarah, Wesley would come to see that there were circumstances where it was appropriate to set aside these injunctions for a higher purpose. He finally made preaching by women the official position of Methodism as seen most clearly in the case of Sarah Mallet—who, at Wesley's urging, was officially sanctioned to preach by the Methodist conference in Manchester, England.

Women preachers have an extraordinary call that fits the extraordinary calling of the people called Methodists. Wesley's concept of an "extraordinary dispensation" allowed him to condone and encourage the place of lay preachers in the movement, despite criticism from the Anglican Church. This same dispensation allowed him to recognize the role of women. Women preachers were not cross-purposed, but fit readily into Wesley's pragmatic ideology of the meaning and means of Methodism; it is clear that Wesley was able to deal with women individually in such a way that they were always affirmed and encouraged to reach their full spiritual potential. He recognized their valuable contribution to his beloved movement.

The Holiness Movement

As Susie Stanley's exceptional book, *Holy Boldness*, shows, hundreds of women began preaching with an empowered sense

---

5. Paul Wesley Chilcote, *John Wesley and the Women Preachers of Early Methodism* (Lanham, MD: Scarecrow Press, 1991), 155.

of self and calling in what came to be known as the Holiness Movement. Phoebe Palmer was a key figure in this movement. Palmer has been cited as an important contributor to the nineteenth-century debate concerning the role of women in the church. In the words of Donald Dayton: "It was . . . the denominations produced by the mid-nineteenth century 'holiness revival' that most consistently raised feminism to a central principle of church life. This movement largely emerged from the work of Phoebe Palmer."[6]

Indeed, Palmer's *The Promise of the Father,* a defense of women in ministry written in 1859, anticipates many of the interpretive moves of twentieth-century feminist exegetes. But it is unlikely that the isolated literary pronouncements of even such a revered founding figure as Phoebe Palmer would themselves be enough to induce an entire religious movement to take such a decisive and controversial stand on the issue of women's roles. Rather, the Holiness Movement's consistently strong endorsement of the equality of women is rooted not only in Palmer's exegesis in *Promise of the Father* but also in her far more influential articulation of the distinctive Holiness doctrine of entire sanctification. To put it simply, Palmer made it possible for women to understand themselves as entirely sanctified and thereby as encouraged to adopt new roles in radical disjunction with their pasts. Nancy Hardesty articulates this separation:

> [Palmer] affirmed that Christians were not only justified before God but were also regenerate, reborn, made new, capable of being restored to the Edenic state. For women it made possible the sweeping away of centuries of patriarchal, misogynist culture in the instant. . . . The argument

---

6. Donald W. Dayton, *Discovering an Evangelical Heritage* (Peabody, MA: Hendrickson, 1988), 200.

that "this is the way we've always done it," holds no power for someone for whom "all things have been made new."[7] This was the primary message of Palmer's theology. She developed a comprehensive theological vision across her writings and preaching that was, and is, especially liberating for women. Palmer's own experience of entire sanctification led her to develop a theological scheme that modified Wesley. The theological modifications she espoused, which resulted from the innovative merging of holiness doctrine with the fervor of American revivalism, catalyzed Palmer to break traditional roles herself, and to emphasize women's unrestricted potential in her preaching and writing.

Persons such as Catherine Booth of the Salvation Army and B. T. Roberts of Free Methodism also wrote treatises on women's right to preach. Roberts wrote *Ordination of Women* in 1891. Cofounder of the Salvation Army, reformer, writer, and preacher Catherine Booth (née Mumford) was born to a Methodist family in England in the early nineteenth century. The family moved to Boston when she was young, where they were heavily involved in the Temperance Movement. Catherine returned to London at the age of fifteen, where she started attending Methodist class meetings. In 1851, she was expelled from the Methodist connection because she favored a group interested in Methodist reform. William Booth was a member of this group. Catherine married him at the age of thirty-six and had eight children. Influenced by Phoebe Palmer, Catherine published *Female Ministry* in 1859, in which she called women to accept and seek all areas of Christian ministry, including preaching; she herself began to preach the following year. With her husband, Catherine established a new branch of

---

7. Nancy Hardesty, Women Called to Witness: Evangelical Feminism in the 19th Century (Nashville: Abingdon Press, 1984), 83.

the Holiness Movement: the Salvation Army, with the doctrine of Christian perfection central to its theology. Out of such theology, the social imperative of reform became central to its religious practice that included the rights of women.

And so, women across North America and Great Britain began to testify in public, standing in mixed assemblies to proclaim God's sanctifying power. Women speaking in public became more common as the century wore on, but Palmer challenged women to testify soon after her own experience in 1837, when public speaking by a woman would have been considered scandalous. Palmer stressed that if a woman were entirely devoted to God, she would be willing to do what God asked of her, even if it went against social norms or protocol. Following this model, the Holiness Movement allowed women to fulfill this special calling of God. Preaching was the next inevitable step after testimony, ordination the next step after preaching. All of this is based on a belief in equality that arises from more than socio-historical factors. Wesleyan-Holiness theology gave rise to practical application. Wesleyan-Holiness women preached from the beginning of the movement, and they continue to preach today.

Two
Wesleyan-Holiness Foundations for Women in Ministry

Rev. Dr. Jacob Lett
Minister and Professor
United States and United Kingdom

Phoebe Palmer asks a question in her book *Promise of the Father*: "When the Spirit was poured out in the answer to the united prayers of God's sons and daughters, did the tongue of fire descend alike upon the women as upon the men?"[1] Since the inception of the Wesleyan-Holiness movement, we have always answered yes to Palmer's question. Women clergy are woven into our fabric. Consider the roles that Phoebe Palmer,

---

1. Phoebe Palmer, *Promise of the Father: Or, A Neglected Speciality of the Last Days. Addressed to the Clergy and Laity of All Christian Communities* (Boston: Henry V. Degen, 1859), 21.

Catherine Booth, and Mildred Bangs Wynkoop played in the formation of our identity.

As Paul Bassett states, "By 1890, then, for most Wesleyan-Holiness people, the ministry of ordained women was as much of the theological and practical fabric of their mission as the doctrine of sin or the practice of congregational singing. . . . Wesleyan-Holiness people generally had decided that concerning the matter of women's ordination, the Spirit has spoken, the case is closed."[2] However, in Bassett's diagnosis, the Spirit's work had been so successful that by the mid-twentieth century the Wesleyan rationale for female ordained ministry had been taken for granted, especially in the Church of the Nazarene. Since this theological position was tacitly assumed, rather than actively taught, a non-Wesleyan spirit and theology crept in, greatly reducing the number of Nazarene women clergy in the second half of the twentieth century.[3]

The key theological foundation for early Wesleyan-Holiness leaders was the concept of apostolic ministry, or "apostolicity." As Stan Ingersol says, "The concept of apostolic ministry—a simple but explosive idea, long since ignored—lay behind this openness to women's voices and gifts."[4] Furthermore, according to Phineas Bresee, the founder of the Church of the Nazarene, the "sole qualification for ordination" is apostolicity.[5] While there are many theologies of apostolicity, three common ele-

---

2. Paul M. Bassett, "The Ordination of Women to Ministry in the Church of the Nazarene," unpublished essay, n.d., https://www.whdl.org/sites/default/files/BASSETT_Ordination%20of%20Women.pdf.

3. Bassett, "The Ordination of Women;" Stan Ingersol, "Your Daughters Shall Prophesy," *Holiness Today* (March/April 2000), https://holinesstoday. org/Your-Daughters-Shall-Prophesy. Ingersol notes that "women pastored more than 230 Nazarene congregations in the United States as late as 1955. By 1985 they pastored only 52."

4. Ingersol, "Your Daughters Shall Prophesy."

5. Bassett, "The Ordination of Women."

ments are found in many of them: continuity, integrity, and calling.[6] The one recited most by early Wesleyans was the Spirit's calling. That is, the Spirit calls and gifts individuals and the church to proclaim the gospel in word and deed (Matthew 28:19–20; Acts 1:8; John 20:21). Christians are considered to be apostolic when they faithfully proclaim the words and actions of the Lord Jesus Christ. This activity for Wesleyans is distinctly tied to the work of the Spirit.[7] For example, Palmer's justification for women in ministry is built on God's promise in Joel 2:28–29, and fulfilled at Pentecost (Acts 2:16–17) to pour out the Spirit on all people, male and female.[8] To summarize, for the early Wesleyans *the descent of the Spirit on all people* was the theological rationale for women proclaiming the gospel alongside men.

This early foundation is further developed in the Nazarene *Manual's* statement "Theology of Women in Ministry," which boldly declares that denying women a place in ministry "violates the spirit and practice of the Wesleyan-Holiness tradition" and "is incompatible with the character of God presented throughout Scripture, especially as revealed in the person of Jesus Christ."[9] Though brief, the *Manual* statement adds to the early focus on the doctrine of the Spirit by considering how the doctrine of Christ also confronts gendered ministry stereotypes. Therefore, relying on early church and Wesleyan theologians, we will show in this chapter how an integration of Christology and pneumatology (the doctrines of Christ and the

---

6. Douglas M. Koskela, "'But Who Laid Hands on Him?' Apostolicity and Methodist Ecclesiology," *Pro Ecclesia* 20.1 (2011), 29, 35.

7. Montague Williams, "What Is the Church?" in *Essential Beliefs: A Wesleyan Primer*, eds. Diane Leclerc and Mark A. Maddix (Kansas City, MO: Beacon Hill Press of Kansas City, 2016), 129–35.

8. Palmer, Promise of the Father, 21–22.

9. Church of the Nazarene *Manual: 2017–2021* (Kansas City, MO: Nazarene Publishing House, 2017), 192.

Spirit) demonstrates that to limit anyone's right to proclaim the gospel because of gender, race, or social status is to erode the very foundation of humanity's salvation. When Christ assumes, redeems, and resurrects human flesh, he confronts those categories by which we normally judge human flesh. When the Spirit descends, the Spirit extends the fundamental reality we have in Christ to our space and time and invites us—all of us—to proclaim the gospel.

The Word Became Flesh:
The Sanctification of Humanity in Christ

For early church theologians and the Wesleyan-Holiness tradition, the focus of the person and work of Christ—Christology—is the sanctification of humanity. One of the issues in Western theology (Roman Catholicism and Protestantism) is an almost exclusive focus on the cross, with little attention given to the incarnation. Of course, we certainly see a focus on the Passion narratives in the Gospels and in the Pauline corpus, but they, as T. A. Noble notes, are not simply about the crucifixion but about the *Christ* who was crucified.[10] Today we are aware of numerous people who have been wrongfully executed, but what separates the *saving* significance of the innocent death of Christ from the innocent deaths of so many other individuals throughout history is the *personhood* of Christ. A cursory reading of any of the major figures throughout theological history (be it Athanasius, Gregory of Nyssa, or Anselm) would show that the *work* of Christ is effective because of *who* Christ is. This essential relationship between salvation (the work of Christ) and Christology (the person of Christ) is especially crucial when considering the work of holiness: sanctification.

---

10. T. A. Noble, Holy Trinity, Holy People: The Historic Doctrine of Christian Perfecting (Eugene, OR: Cascade Books, 2013), 158–59.

The sanctification of humanity—our ultimate union with the triune God of love—is possible because of Christ's "assumption" (taking on) of the human "flesh" (our corporate condition marked by sin, suffering, and death). When Christ was born of Mary (Galatians 4:4), he related himself to the human nature we all have. Standard orthodox Christology asserts that Christ must be "fully human." As it says in Hebrews, Christ was "fully human in every way"—"yet he did not sin" (2:17; 4:15). By becoming fully human in every way, Christ—the eternal Word—became the Savior of all of humanity.

Scripture and tradition describe the incarnation as a "great exchange" between Christ's humanity and divinity. Second Corinthians 8:9 states, "For you know the grace of our Lord Jesus Christ, that though he was rich, yet for your sake he became poor, so that you through his poverty might become rich." Christ died to the old creation, to our decaying flesh, so that we might arise with him in the new creation (Romans 6:5–11; Ephesians 4:22–24). The great doctors of the church summarized this exchange between Christ's divinity and humanity this way: Christ became human so humanity might participate in the life of God. In more Wesleyan terms, Christ, the Holy One, became human so humans might become holy. Some of the most famous words handed down by the Christian tradition are from Gregory of Nazianzus, who states that if Christ did not assume our humanity, then we would remain "unhealed," or unsanctified. This theology is reflected in one of Charles Wesley's hymns: "He deigns in flesh t'appear/ Widest extremes to join/To bring our vileness near/And make us all divine."[11] In Scripture and tradition, there is this wonderful exchange between the poverty, brokenness, decay, and death of

---

11. Quoted in Noble, *Holy Trinity, Holy People*, 171–72.

the human nature we share with Christ and the riches, beauty, and holiness of the divine nature Christ offers to share with us.[12] What concerns us here is if there was a particular *kind* of human nature that Christ became. It seems that if Christ only assumed a male nature and was our Savior as a man, then only men are invited into the mystery of sanctification. In fact, there are examples throughout church history where Christ's maleness is used as the rationale for an exclusively male priesthood.[13] Let's follow this logic for a moment. If we start speaking of *one* particular property of Christ's human nature, then we also need to consider other properties of that nature. For example, Christ was a *Jewish* man; so should only *Jewish men* be priests? One question early Christian theologians had to address was how a Jewish Messiah could save gentiles. Orthodox Christology, however, did not put the focus on Jesus's particular human characteristics (his maleness, his Jewishness) but on his relation to corporate humanity—to the whole human species.[14] In Scripture, it is clear that the focus is on how Christ relates to *all* of humanity (two keys texts are Romans 5:12–21 and 1 Corinthians 15:20–23, 45–49). As it says in 1 Corinthians 15:22, "For as in Adam all die, so in Christ all will be made alive." Noble states, "The Son of God thus sanctifies *our*

---

12. For a more thorough summary of the relationship between Christ, humanity, and sanctification, see Noble, *Holy Trinity*, 158–72.

13. For a classic work on how Christian doctrine has been used to oppress women, see Rosemary Radford Ruether, *Sexism and God-Talk: Toward a Feminist Theology* (Boston: Beacon Press, 1983).

14. Gregory of Nyssa, *Catechetical Discourse: A Handbook for Catechists*, trans. Ignatius Green (Yonkers, NY: St. Vladimir's Seminary Press, 2019), 130–31. Frances M. Young notes, "The humanity of Christ is some kind of corporate whole, and Athanasius's entire theological schema would fail if it were not so." See Francis M. Young, "Adam and Christ: Human Solidarity before God" in *The Christian Doctrine of Humanity: Explorations in Constructive Dogmatics*, Oliver D. Crisp and Fred Sanders, ed. (Grand Rapids: Zondervan, 2018), 150.

common, corporate humanity by uniting it to his own Person in being born as a human being from Mary by action of the Sanctifying Spirit."[15]

Of course, it would be impossible for Jesus to become all the particularities of humanity in order to save and sanctify them. For example, how could Jesus simultaneously have blonde *and* black hair? Likewise, how can Jesus simultaneously be both male *and* female? If we make salvation dependent on Jesus's relation to *every* human characteristic, then the majority of humans would remain distant from God. As Ian McFarland says, "Jesus's role as Savior requires neither that he exhibit any particular human trait (e.g., maleness rather than femaleness), nor that he be superior to other human beings with respect to any particular human capacity (as, e.g., the strongest, swiftest, or smartest human being who ever lived)."[16] Jesus is fully human simply by being an ordinary human with particular human characteristics.

To sum up this brief overview of the relationship between Christology and sanctification, Jesus may have been a Jewish male born in a particular place and time, but for Scripture and tradition, that reality does not limit salvation only to male Jewish believers. Christ is human in the fullest sense. And it is his ordinary and corporate humanity that is united to God in his incarnation and extended to people of various kinds at Pentecost.

When the Spirit Descends: The Unity of Humanity

The means by which we participate in the universally redeemed and sanctified humanity of the Lord Jesus Christ is the Spirit. First John 4:13 states, "This is how we know that we live in him and he in us: He has given us of his Spirit."

---

15. Noble, *Holy Trinity*, 170.

16. Ian A. McFarland, *The Word Made Flesh: A Theology of the Incarnation* (Louisville: Westminster John Knox Press, 2019), 128–29.

The early church theologians' summative phrase to describe sanctification is that it is completed "by the Son in the Spirit".[17] While Christian holiness is the objective work of Christ—it is completed by Christ *pro nobis* ("for us")—Pentecost reminds us that this completed act works itself out in the community of God's people in the Spirit. The Spirit is the presence of Christ here and now, uniting, re-creating, and sanctifying our times, places, and bodies according to that which began in Christ.

Wesleyan-Holiness theologians have relied on the account of Pentecost in Acts to substantiate why all human beings—male and female—are invited to proclaim the gospel. Furthermore, as seen in their official statements on the ordination of women, many Wesleyan-Holiness denominations connect Pentecost to Galatians 3:26–28. When the Spirit is poured out "on all people" (Acts 2:17), the result is that "there is neither Jew nor Gentile, neither slave nor free, nor is there male and female, for you are all one in Christ Jesus" (Galatians 3:28). The Church of the Nazarene's *Manual* statement says it this way: "The purpose of Christ's redemptive work is to set God's creation free from the curse of the fall. Those who are 'in Christ' are new creations (2 Corinthians 5:17). In this redemptive community, no human being is to be regarded as inferior on the basis of social status, race, or gender (Galatians 3:26–28)."[18]

While some argue that Galatians 3 only refers to *spiritual* unity and thus should not be used to support the case for women in ministry, Catherine Booth asks, "If this passage does not teach that in the privileges, duties, and responsibilities of Christ's kingdom, all differences of nation, caste, and sex are abolished, we should like to know what it does teach,

---

17. Thomas Weinandy, The Father's Spirit of Sonship: Reconceiving the Trinity (Edinburgh: T & T Clark, 1995).

18. Church of the Nazarene, *Manual: 2017–2021*, 192.

and wherefore it was written."[19] Merely spiritual interpretations of Galatians 3 do not fall within the framework of Holiness people, who believe that the Spirit extends our spiritual state in Christ to our day-to-day embodied life as workers for the kingdom of God.[20]

We can see how, for Wesleyan-Holiness theology, hierarchical differences that are justified on the basis of natural differences like gender are not the *order* of creation given by God but the *curse* of sin, which seeks to fragment rather than unify humanity. The hierarchical relationship between male and female is a consequence of the fall. The original design is that humanity—together being made in the image of God as male and female—would *together* take responsibility for God's creation (Genesis 1:26–28). Holiness people, understanding Pentecost to be a reversal of the fall, believe that the consequences of sin are redeemed by Christ and being healed by the Spirit as humanity is made into a new creation (2 Corinthians 5:17).[21] Therefore, in the descent at Pentecost, the Spirit begins the work of sanctifying and unifying humanity, the very thing Jesus prayed for in John 17:17–23. Therefore, hierarchical relations based on gender, race, or social class are in opposition to

---

19. Quoted in Paul W. Chilcote, *The Methodist Defense of Women in Ministry: A Documentary History* (Eugene, OR: Cascade Books, 2017), 143.

20. For the relationship between holiness and practice in the Wesleyan tradition, see Diane Leclerc, *Discovering Christian Holiness: The Heart of Wesleyan-Holiness Theology* (Kansas City, MO: Beacon Hill Press of Kansas City, 2010), 277–79.

21. Kristina LaCelle-Peterson, "The Church as Egalitarian Liberator" in *Essential Church: A Wesleyan Ecclesiology*, ed. Diane Leclerc and Mark A. Maddix (Kansas City, MO: Beacon Hill Press of Kansas City, 2014), 150. It is significant to note that the early church understood Pentecost to be the reversal of Babel, as is reflected in Orthodox liturgy: "When the Most High came down and confounded tongues of men at Babel, he divided the nations. When he dispensed the tongues of fire, he called all to unity, and with one voice we glorify the Most Holy Spirit" (Kontakion for Pentecost).

the work of the Spirit, who seeks to liberate humans from such distorted power structures, to unify us, and to make us holy.

Christ Has Spoken:
All Are Called and Gifted for Ministry

When the Church of the Nazarene boldly declares that denying women a place in ministry "violates the spirit and practice of the Wesleyan-Holiness tradition" and "is incompatible with the character of God presented throughout Scripture, especially as revealed in the person of Jesus Christ,"[22] it is calling the community of God's people to repent and reorder the mindset around the incarnate ministry of the Lord Jesus Christ. When Jesus begins his ministry in the Gospel of Matthew, he says, "Repent, for the kingdom of heaven has come near" (4:17). The Greek word for "repent" is *metanoia*, which means to change both your mind and your actions. When we encounter the God revealed in Christ, it should transform our mindsets (Romans 12:2)—this is part of the sanctifying process. One of the primary areas that the gospel seems keen to transform is our perception of who holds power and on what basis they hold power, as is poignantly evident in Christ's teaching on the Beatitudes (Matthew 5:1–12) and in the kinds of people he associated with.

When the Spirit descends, the Spirit extends Christ's ministry to the life of his people. What begins in Jerusalem is to be spread to the ends of the earth (Acts 1:8).

When the Spirit descends, the Spirit confronts our inherited social, political, and biological demarcations. The Spirit challenges us to have them transformed according to our more fundamental reality, a reality that is in Christ and spread abroad through the gifts of the Spirit.

---

22. Church of the Nazarene, *Manual: 2017–2021*, 192.

When the Spirit descends, the Spirit calls us to the universal priesthood of believers, to the apostolic ministry (1 Peter 2:5). The Spirit falls upon all, calling them to the ministry of service and uniquely gifting them to serve in particular areas of ministry (Ephesians 4:11).[23]

The fruit of such Spirit-filled transformation is seen in early Wesleyan-Holiness churches. For example, in 1890 Phineas Bresee employed Amanda Smith, who had been enslaved, to preach at a revival. Listen to how Bresee describes her preaching: "She preached one Sabbath afternoon, as I never heard her preach before, and as I have rarely ever heard anybody preach, in strains of holy eloquence and unction, almost equal to Bishop Simpson in the zenith of his power and sacred oratory. The Lord opened heaven on the people in mighty tides of glory."[24] Bresee recognized and affirmed that Smith's eloquent preaching was in fact an event of the Spirit that echoed Pentecost.

When the Spirit descends, all are called to and gifted for ministry (1 Corinthians 12:4–31; 14:1–19; Romans 12:3–8; Ephesians 4:7–16; 1 Peter 4:8–11). While this fact is indisputable, the key question in the debate of women in ministry is whether human social markers like gender can exclude a person from a particular type of pastoral service, like ordained ministry. Although there are two controversial passages in the New Testament (discussed in detail in chapter 4), the answer—according to the Wesleyan-Holiness emphasis on the doctrines of Christ and the Spirit—is no. The fundamental judgment or mark of any human being is first and foremost that they are in

---

23. As LaCelle-Peterson argues, "Roles in this new community are based on the gifts given by the Holy Spirit, not on social markers imported from the cultures in which the church functions." See LaCelle-Peterson, "The Church as Egalitarian Liberator," 152.

24. Quoted in E. A. Girvin, *Phineas F. Bresee: A Prince in Israel, A Biography* (Kansas City, MO: Pentecostal Nazarene Publishing House, 1916), 91.

Christ, and the Spirit extends our status in Christ by calling, gifting, and gracing us to proclaim the gospel. The only basis on which one might be denied a place in ministry is when a body of church leaders carefully and patiently discerns that a person does not have the Spirit-given call, gifts, and graces for a particular type of ministry. For Wesleyan-Holiness people, to deny anyone a place in ministry for reasons other than this—be it because of gender, race, or social status—is to deny the work of Christ in the Spirit.[25]

In light of the scriptural narrative of salvation, the great irony here is that, by denying women a place to serve, male gentiles implicitly deny their own right to serve God *as gentiles*. All humans are to be evaluated by the same criteria—criteria that are not marked by the social norms of any one particular culture but by the sanctified humanity of Christ and the Spirit's call, gifts, and graces. We have already noted Paul Bassett's statement that, when it comes to women's place in ordained ministry in the Wesleyan-Holiness tradition, "the Spirit has spoken, the case is closed." Let us add: Christ has spoken, the case is closed.

25. H. Orton Wiley, *Christian Theology*, vol. III (Kansas City, MO: Beacon Hill Press, 1943), 127–29.

Three
The Place of Women in Ministry in the New Testament

Rev. Dr. Svetlana Khobnya
Minister and Professor
Russia and United Kingdom

Paul has often been portrayed as a man who prohibited women from serving in positions of church leadership. Pointing to passages of Scripture that can be taken out of context and read in a negative light has become the focus of so many. What has been lost in this conversation is the positive threads woven throughout the New Testament—in the Gospels, the writings of Paul, and other epistles. One cannot simply read particular passages of Scripture without contemplating the whole. If we do that, we may be left asking whether there are any passages in the New Testament that affirm women in ministry.

My friend once returned from a conference and shared with me her experience of listening to a reading of Romans 16. She was surprised to notice not only the number of women listed in this chapter but also the description of the ministerial roles they fulfilled alongside Paul and other men in the church. Romans 16 may not be a popular text to read for devotional purposes or at public gatherings, but it is one more piece of evidence in the New Testament that highlights the various roles women fulfilled in the early church. Let us recall Junia,[1] who is named as an apostle by Paul himself (16:7); Phoebe, who was a deacon/minister (Greek, *diakonos*[2]) of the church and a benefactor of many, including Paul (vv. 1–2); Priscilla, who worked with Paul alongside her husband, Aquila (v. 3), and taught the "way of God" in synagogues, where early Jewish Christians continued to meet (Acts 18:24–26). Mary (Romans 16:6), Tryphena, Tryphosa and Persis (16:12) also served in churches.

In addition to these and other individually named women, the New Testament is full of other female characters who play significant roles in the early church.[3] In fact, if we attempt to read the New Testament in one go—paying attention to female characters, as Linda Belleville suggests—we will hardly be able

---

1. In some translations—for example, the old NASB (1995)—this name is rendered in the masculine as Junias, even though commentators before the thirteenth century were almost unanimously in favour of the feminine identification. Junia was a common Latin name, and there is no evidence of Junias used as a masculine name. See Douglas J. Moo, *The New International Commentary on the New Testament: The Epistle to the Romans* (Grand Rapids: William B. Eerdmans Publishing Company, 1996), 938.

2. The Greek word *diakonos* could mean either "deacon" or "minister," but since Paul is addressing people in the church, the term most likely refers to the office of responsibility the person holds. James Dunn believes Phoebe is "the first recorded 'deacon' in church history." James D. G. Dunn, *Word Biblical Commentary 38b: Romans 9–16* (Dallas: Word Books, 1988), 887.

3. See a comprehensive list in Carol Meyers, Toni Craven, and Ross S. Kraemer, eds., *Women in Scripture: A Dictionary of Named and Unnamed Women in the Hebrew Bible, the Apocryphal/Deuterocanonical Books, and New Testament* (New York: Houghton Mifflin, 2000).

to move from one book to the next without the mention of a woman prophet (Acts 21:9; 1 Corinthians 11:5), evangelist (Philippians 4:2–3), teacher (Acts 18:26; Titus 2:3–5), patron (Romans 16:2), or prayer leader (1 Timothy 5:5).[4]

If Scripture provides so much evidence to demonstrate that women have always participated in ministry alongside men, why does the question still arise? Perhaps we like to focus on some passages while ignoring others. Possibly we like to read our own convictions and presuppositions into the text without allowing the text to speak to us. Or it may be that we are so focused on a certain passage or even certain words in a passage that we forget to look at the wider context or the whole narrative—of which these passages are only a part. While it may take volumes to provide a comprehensive and biblically sound response to a variety of opinions about women in ministry, let us confine ourselves to an overview of the New Testament story as a whole. The purpose of this chapter is to analyze the extent to which the New Testament affirms the position of women as equal to men in relation to serving together in any capacity for the sake of the gospel. Feasibly, this analysis will allow us to offer some counterarguments to those who have opposing views.

Overview of Scriptural Evidence

Any treatment of the New Testament starts with the recognition that the New Testament is the story of the fulfillment of God's promises to his people and the story of the restoration of relationships between God, humanity, and the rest of creation in Christ. If human disobedience resulted in broken relationships, including a gender dysfunction (Genesis

---

4. Linda L. Belleville, "Women in Ministry: An Egalitarian Perspective" in Linda L. Bellville, Craig L. Blomberg, Craig S. Keener, and Thomas R. Schreiner, *Two Views on Women in Ministry, Revised Edition* (Grand Rapids: Zondervan, 2005), 35.

3:16) that presented a shift from the divine intent of partnership and responsible co-dominion over the earth (Genesis 1–2), then in Christ Jesus these relationships are restored (Galatians 3:28). The sad fact that gender hierarchy remains an issue in the world "does indicate something of the direction to which human nature will incline, given the encouragement."[5] There are examples in the Old Testament of women who, when the opportunity is given, reach extraordinary positions in public life (such as Deborah and Esther). We learn of prophetically gifted women like Miriam and Huldah (Exodus 15:20–21; 2 Kings 22:14–20)—religious leaders and speakers for the Lord.

However, Jesus is the first one, according to the Gospel writers, to raise the status of *all* women. Jesus's life and ministry demonstrate his mission to women, even in the face of breaking Jewish custom. He speaks both to women (John 4:27) and on their behalf (Mark 12:40). He breaks the Sabbath on behalf of a sick woman and restores her to a proper social status (Luke 13:10–17). Women play a significant role throughout his ministry and also in his genealogy.[6] Moreover, Jesus liberates both men and women for mission and discipleship (Luke 10:1–23)[7] and encourages the community of his followers to be

---

5. Belleville, "Women in Ministry," 31.

6. See Richard Bauckham, *Gospel Women: Studies of the Named Women in the Gospels* (Grand Rapids: William B. Eerdmans Publishing Company, 2002).

7. Some deny the possibility that women are included in the group of the seventy-two sent out on mission. See, for example, John F. MacArthur, *Twelve Ordinary Men: How the Master Shaped His Disciples for Greatness, and What He Wants to Do with You* (Nashville: Thomas Nelson, 2002). MacArthur is an advocate for restrictive roles for women in general. However, women play a prominent role in the life and mission of Jesus and disciples. They are portrayed as righteous and trusting in God—at times, more trusting in God than some male characters (for example, Luke juxtaposes Zechariah, who does not believe the angel at first, with Mary, who obeys at once in 1:20, 38). Luke presents women as true servants of the Lord and

a light for all the people (Matthew 5:16). Jesus motivates a Samaritan woman to become an evangelist in her village despite her doubtful reputation (John 4:7–42). He reinforces Mary's position as a disciple at his feet (Luke 10:38–42). Although there are no female disciples among the Twelve, the Gospel writers report that there are women traveling from place to place with Jesus. They support him and the rest of the disciples with their resources (Luke 8:1–4). The imperfect tenses used in the narratives indicate the ongoing activity of these women ministering to Jesus (Mark 15:41; Luke 8:3). Let us not forget that women were the first witnesses to the reality of the empty tomb and, as such, the first preachers of the gospel.

In fact, the whole idea of discipleship needs a fresh look, and recognition of its deeper sense in the Gospels. Some have noted that the significance of various characters in the narrative is determined not by the frequency with which they appear but by their thematic contribution. What happens if we reexamine the idea of discipleship within the narrative framework and ask the question of how particular characters engage with Jesus throughout the Gospels? The appearance of women in the Gospel of Mark, for example, and their interactions with Jesus demonstrate a specific pattern that can be observed in other Gospels as well (Mark 1:29–31; 5:24–34; 7:24–30; 14:3–9; 15:40–41, 47; 16:1–8). Markan female characters not only accept but also participate in God's transformative reality. These women demonstrate faithfulness and service, extending Mark's theological portrait of discipleship. In some situations, male disciples fail Jesus—for example, they fail to cast out a demon when the authority is given to them, or they sleep when Jesus asks them to stay awake (Mark 9:14–29; 14:32–42). In

---

missionaries of the gospel. As such, they are meant to be part of those who are sent on mission. See Jerome H. Neyrey, *The Social World of Luke–Acts: Models for Interpretation* (Peabody, MA: Hendrickson Publishers, 1991), 262.

contrast, the women collectively create "a trajectory of faithfulness" and reflect "the way in which God's kingdom renews creation and redefines humanity in the image of Christ."[8] These women contribute to and complete the Gospel's vision of embodied discipleship. This vision is not about who the disciples are (whether men or women) but about a dynamic activity of both men and women that "requires an active embodiment of the transformative reality of God's kingdom and a faithful allegiance to the crucified and resurrected Jesus."[9]

The book of Acts provides further names of women in ministry. Mary, the mother of John, hosts a house church in Jerusalem (Acts 12:12). The early Christians routinely gathered at the homes of prominent believers for worship. Unfortunately, we do not know much about Mary, the host of this house church mentioned in Acts, and some argue that being a host does not necessarily mean pastoring, shepherding, or overseeing a congregation.[10] However, as the host, she certainly would have carried the responsibility for the people gathered in her space, and being the host, even if it does not automatically mean she oversaw the congregation, also does not automatically exclude that possibility. She would then have been one of a few female overseers of early churches mentioned in the New Testament (Colossians 4:15).

We know a little more about another house church hostess in Acts. Lydia, a businesswoman from a town near Philippi, converted to Christianity during Paul's visit to the city and opened her home to Christian fellowship (Acts 16:14–15). Paul

---

8. Jeffrey W. Aernie, *Narrative Discipleship: Portraits of Women in the Gospel of Mark* (Eugene, OR: Pickwick Publications, 2018), 120.

9. Aernie, Narrative Discipleship, 5.

10. Craig S. Keener and Thomas R. Schreiner argue this point in their responses to Belleville's egalitarian perspective presented in "Women in Ministry," 106, 112.

and those with him went back to Lydia's house after they were released from prison (v. 40). From Paul's letter to the Philippians we learn that the church there not only survived but actually flourished. We can be certain Lydia was one of the pillars of Christianity there, included in the list of saints in Philippi (Philippians 1:1–7). She must have been one of those "co-workers, whose names are in the book of life," laboring with Paul for the sake of the gospel (Philippians 4:3).

Acts presents the story of the restorative activity of the Spirit who was promised to the sons and daughters of God beforehand in the prophets (Joel 2:28–29), and now is being poured out upon all flesh (Acts 2:16–21). Now men and women together prophesy about the Messiah, and devote themselves to the apostles' teaching and fellowship (Acts 2:14–47; 21:9). The early church successfully wins men and women—who are called brothers and sisters, who receive the gift of the Holy Spirit, and who share worship life together (Acts 1:4; 16:13–40; 17:4, 12).

Women in general are part of worship communities sharing the same gifts and ministering together with men as one body (1 Corinthians 11:4–5; 12). For example, Paul refers to men as his coworkers (Romans 16:2, 9, 21; 1 Corinthians 3:9; 16:16–17; 2 Corinthians 8:23; Philippians 2:25; 4:3; Colossians 4:11; 1 Thessalonians 3:2; Philippians 1:24), as hard workers (1 Corinthians 4:12; 16:16), and as those who have risked their lives for him (Romans 16:4). But he uses the same language for women: as coworkers (Romans 16:3–4; Philippians 4:3), as hard workers (Romans 16:6, 12), and as those who have risked their lives for him (Romans 16:4). In addition to women in leadership positions mentioned in Romans 16, Paul also greets Nympha, the overseer of the house church in Laodicea (Colossians 4:15). In 1 Corinthians 11:5, Paul clearly states that women are prophesying just like men in the church worship service. The dress code seems to be different for men and women in Paul's day, but the gift of prophecy is not gender-restrictive. In 1 Corinthians 14, Paul also sounds inclusive of men and women when he explains how to organize worship and prophecy (vv. 26, 31). Pursuing his call in Christ, Paul invites others to be of the same mind, and asks others to help Euodia and Syntyche, his female co-companions who labor alongside him in the ministry of the gospel, to resolve their differences for the sake of the gospel (Philippians 4:2–3). All these examples testify to the fact that male and female disciples served in Paul's churches. There is no doubt that Paul, as the main New Testament letter writer to churches, is open to women in ministry and leadership.

Some challenging New Testament passages may obscure our understanding of Paul's view of the role of women in the church—for example, 1 Corinthians 14:34–35 and 1 Timothy 2:8–15. These and other passages need special attention and are dealt with in chapter 4.[11] Suffice it to say that these passages draw a complex picture of particular situations, and it is doubtful they prescribe a relationship between men and women as rulers and subjects. Moreover, these challenging passages need to be studied within a wider New Testament framework: Paul and other New Testament writers emphasize that in churches the matter of relationships is one of unity in diversity. Women, like men, worship publicly, exercise their gifts in the church, and have leadership positions. If women are uneducated (which would be true for many women at that time), then they are encouraged to learn so they can continue their Christian walk with men in faith and love and holiness (1 Timothy 2:11, 15). "Let a woman learn" are crucial words in the New Testament

11. See also Svetlana Khobnya, "Preparing Women for Ministry in 1 Cor 14:34–35 and 1 Tim 2:8–15," *Didache*, Vol. 19, No. 1 (February 2020), https://didache.nazarene.org/index.php/volume-19.

that call women to education, encouraging them to reach their full potential in order to be equipped for ministry.

In some texts, Christian women are asked to be subordinate to their unbelieving husbands (who most likely follow the post-fall perception of sexual hierarchy) so that they may be won over for the gospel (1 Peter 3:1). Such a family dynamic is far from a Christian model, though. Christian men are already expected to be transformed. They are to demonstrate love and honor. This model of love and respect toward women is the only way for Christian men to stand right in relationship to God. Then men's prayers will not be hindered, says Peter (1 Peter 3:7).[12] Together, Christian men and women are to practice unity of spirit, love, and humility (among other virtues) toward each other (1 Peter 3:8). Practically, there is no place for slavery, misuse, suppression, or violence when there are love, hospitality, service to each other, and humility. These constitute the lifestyle and true pattern for the church (1 Peter 5:1–5; Philippians 2:3–4). Such an attitude should result in a positive and hopeful picture for ministry: gifted men and women who believe in Christ, know his suffering, and preach his glory can minister in the church in any position in unity of spirit, love, and humility.

Other Perspectives and Conclusion

Of course, not all share this perspective. There are two main views opposing women in ministry that could be challenged in light of the evidence we have gathered in this study.

First, there is a conviction that women in general are understood to be in permanent subordination to men since cre-

---

12. This idea is supported by a number of commentators. See, for example, Paul J. Achtemeier, *1 Peter: A Commentary on 1 Peter. Hermeneia: A Critical and Historical Commentary on the Bible* (Minneapolis: Fortress Press, 1996), 218.

ation.[13] This view considers women to be ontologically inferior to men. Therefore, women are not allowed to teach men under any circumstance. The representatives of this perspective focus on the passages that help them explain women's subordination—for example, that women were created second[14] and are more liable to error and deception than men.[15] They downplay other references to women's liberation, leadership, and service. Sadly, according to this view, Christ did not change anything in relation to women's status. Even the explanation of women's salvation is confusing in this perspective. On one hand, salvation is through faith only, but on the other it remains through childbearing.

The second opposing view is complementarianism, which considers women equal to men in receiving salvation. In this view, Christ's salvific action reaches men and women and restores them equally. Women are not to be inferior to men ontologically. But functionally, they are still subordinate to men. In other words, when it comes to leadership, they are not equal. According to this view, God restricts women from serving in church as leaders and instead calls women to serve only in complementary roles. Proponents of this view focus on 1 Timothy 2:12, insisting that women cannot be leaders because they cannot teach or have authority over men. Representatives of this view still allow women to speak and teach groups of men and

---

13. This view was dominant at some point in history, but it is waning now. See a summary in Kevin Giles, "A Critique of the 'Novel' Contemporary Interpretation of 1 Timothy 2:9–15 Given in the Book, *Women in the Church*. Part I," *The Evangelical Quarterly* 72:2 (2000), 151–167.

14. The custom of primogeniture was already repeatedly rejected in the Old Testament (Gen 25:23; 48:19; 49:4), and generally is not helpful for the argument of leadership.

15. The blame for sin has been variously explained in the Jewish tradition and is challenged by Paul, who at one point traces it to Adam, through whom sin enters the world (Romans 5:12).

women but only occasionally, recognizing that the final authority in the church must be male.[16] They approach any other New Testament passages that point to women in ministry from the same premise of role differentiation: women can help or lead but only up to a point (women are not allowed to be elders). Some complementarians, though, are more willing to submit to women leaders in the home, in the church, and in any other context. They are open to rereading Scripture faithfully, recognizing that they might be wrong.[17]

Contrary to the above views, this study offers an egalitarian perspective. Egalitarians point to multiple examples found in Scripture of women in leadership. We argue that, in a redemptive community, such as what is introduced in the New Testament, no human being is rendered functionally or ontologically inferior on the basis of gender (or status or race). Neither salvation nor service to Christ is restricted in any way, for men or women. Followers of Christ contribute to the church based on their varied gifts, not on their gender. Egalitarians focus not only on certain passages but also on the totality of scriptural evidence that testifies to God—who, in Christ and Spirit, calls both men and women to lead the church.

---

16. See, for example, Thomas R. Schreiner, "Women in Ministry: Another Complementarian Perspective," *Two Views on Women in Ministry*, 263–322.

17. Craig L. Blomberg, "Women in Ministry: A Complementarian Perspective," *Two Views on Women in Ministry*, 123–84.

Four

Tackling the Challenging Passages in the New Testament

Rev. Dr. C. Jeanne Orjala Serrão
Minister and Professor
United States

There has always been uncertainty and hostility toward women in leadership in Christian circles. Can a Christian woman be in leadership? Shouldn't a woman always be under the authority of a man? These attitudes hinder and sometimes prevent the ministry of women who are called by God to lead. This uncertainty stems partly from some biblical passages that have been taken out of context and used as proof-texts. When we carefully exegete God's Word, the truth overcomes our cultural biases to show us that, just as God created humankind to care for God's creation, so also has God ordained humankind—both male and female—to take leadership roles in society and the church.

Most of the passages used to oppose women in ministry leadership are from Paul. Since Paul's letters make up much of the New Testament, it is important to understand his general principles regarding women in the church. The theme verse related to gender and ethnic diversity in the body of Christ is Galatians 3:28, as previous chapters in this book have established: "There is neither Jew nor Gentile, neither slave nor free, nor is there male and female, for you are all one in Christ Jesus." Some say this verse only refers to spiritual access to God, but these distinctions reflect the basic social divisions of the first century. The conflict between Peter and Paul in Galatians 2:11–14 indicates that the distinction Paul makes in Galatians 3—"neither Jew nor Gentile"—has significant social implications. Paul asks Philemon to treat his runaway slave, Onesimus, "no longer as a slave, but better than a slave, as a dear brother" (Philemon 1:16). Paul does not abolish slavery, but he sows the seeds of its destruction.

In 1 Corinthians 7:3–5—counter to first-century culture, where the woman was to be submissive in all things—Paul confirms that the sexual relationship between a husband and wife is a matter of mutual respect and rights. In 1 Corinthians 11:11–12, in the middle of describing proper worship, Paul declares the interdependence of men and women and in verse 13 allows local churches to decide what type of dress would best express the restored relationship between genders. In addition to the equality and unity of all Christians, Paul also sets out in Ephesians 5:21 the principle of *mutual* submission, to which he holds both men and women accountable. Throughout his letters, Paul also mentions twelve women coworkers by name. These examples, drawn from a variety of New Testament sources, confirm that the proclamation in Galatians 3:28 has social as well as spiritual implications.

Some of the arguments against women in ministry leadership begin with poor, or heavily biased, translations. For instance, Phoebe is called a *diakonon* ("deacon, servant, or minister") of the church in Cenchrea according to Romans 16:1. Most traditional English translations have rendered this as "servant," including the KJV and NASB. However, in 1 Timothy 4:6, the KJV and NIV translate the exact same word (*diakonos*) as "minister" in reference to Timothy. With no obvious explanation or basis for this difference in translation between Romans and 1 Timothy, the main reason appears to reveal a gender bias. Of course, there is no way to be certain of what Paul means when he uses the word in Romans to describe Phoebe. According to William Greathouse and George Lyons, *diakonon* "may designate [Phoebe] generically as a member of a special leadership group within the church."[1] Likewise, however, there is no reason to conclude that Paul considers Timothy and Phoebe to be different kinds of leaders in the church, since he uses the exact same Greek word to describe them both.

In Romans 16, Paul greets Andronicus and Junia (*Iounian*), "my fellow Jews who have been in prison with me. They are outstanding among the apostles, and they were in Christ before I was" (v. 7). Junia's gender cannot be definitely determined from the Greek in this instance, so we examine other historical context from the same era. There is no evidence that this name existed in any form as a man's name in the first century, but there is ample evidence it existed as a woman's name. In the fourth century, church father John Chrysostom understood

---

1. William M. Greathouse with George Lyons, *Romans 9–16: A Commentary in the Wesleyan Tradition*, New Beacon Bible Commentary (Kansas City, MO: Beacon Hill Press of Kansas City, 2008), 265. See also C. E. B. Cranfield, *A Critical and Exegetical Commentary on the Epistle to the Romans, Volume II: Commentary on Romans IX–XVI and Essays* (London: T & T Clark, 1979), 781.

the reference to be to a woman.[2] However, later church leaders could not accept that a woman would be called an apostle—let alone an outstanding apostle—so today many translations and commentaries reflect that bias.

Six Principles for Interpretation

As we address the culturally bound proof-texts that are used to exclude women from leadership positions in ministry, let us keep in mind six basic principles that can help us interpret difficult biblical texts.

Principle #1: Let scriptural passages that are already clear illuminate and interpret ambiguous passages.

Principle #2: Interpret texts in light of their historical and literary contexts.

Principle #3: Be consistent.

Principle #4: Examine the history of the interpretation of the passage.

Principle #5: Ask how experience, tradition, and reason inform the passage.

Principle #6: Pray, study, read, and discuss a difficult passage over a period of months and years. The Spirit can change minds and hearts that are open to transformation.

Tackling the Misunderstood Passages

A few cloudy and misunderstood passages have been used to exclude women from leadership positions in ministry. Some of them are hard to understand because they do not make sense in light of the rest of Scripture. Other passages have been intentionally removed from and interpreted without their proper context in order to fit a particular agenda, worldview, or bias. Let's address these difficult passages.

2. Cranfield, *Romans, Volume II*, 788.

Ephesians 5: Submission and Headship in Marriage

Those who use Ephesians 5:22 against women leaders need to realize that the theme for this passage is clearly stated in 5:21: "Submit to one another out of reverence for Christ." This passage is about the importance of the *mutual* submission of believers. Paul then gives examples of what that looks like in different relationships. He and his coworkers were trying to Christianize a first-century Mediterranean culture that was very suspicious of strong, leading women. For example, Plutarch (AD 46–120) wrote disparagingly about Cleopatra in *Life of Mark Antony*, calling this remarkable, intelligent woman who spoke most of the world's known languages and could outthink many of the male rulers of her time "bewitching," a "flatterer," and dangerous because she was wealthy and highly educated.[3] These were the types of cultural assumptions about women that Paul was working against.

Ephesians 5 begins with the command to imitate God and "walk in the way of love" that shows itself as mutual submission. The use of *agape* in this verse is countercultural. This type of love breaks down barriers of status and gender, and emphasizes mutual loyalty and commitment. The author of Ephesians begins chapter 5 with encouragement to "follow God's example" and "walk in the way of *agape*, just as Christ loved us and gave himself up for us as a fragrant offering and sacrifice to God" (vv. 1–2). This opening sets the context for relationships between believers. As if this were not strong enough, the author then says in verse 21, just before getting specific about different relationships, "Submit to one another out of reverence for Christ."

---

3. Amy Crawford, "Who Was Cleopatra? Mythology, Propaganda, Liz Taylor and the Real Queen of the Nile," *Smithsonian Magazine*, March 31, 2007, https://www.smithsonianmag.com/history/who-was-cleopatra-151356013/.

The love described here voluntarily submits to the other in the same way that Christ submitted himself to the cross.

Because Christ's example of submission is the definition of Christian love and the verb "submit" appears in verse 21, the author does not need to restate the verb in verse 22 (and does not do so in the Greek). That is how we know that the submission encouraged in verse 22 of wives to their husbands is the same submission demanded of *every* Christian to every other Christian. Submission of wives to husbands was, of course, expected during this era, but the command to do it here carries a different implication. Women were seen as intellectually and morally inferior, but they are not being treated that way in this scripture. They are being addressed as Christians who are walking in the way of Christ, and they are encouraged to submit voluntarily to their husbands—*who are their equals.* This voluntary submission—of a woman, to a fellow Christian, who happens to be her husband—is a demonstration of *agape* love. The author completes the statement on love and submission in marriage with the command to the husbands in verse 25. They are to *agapate* their wives "just as Christ loved [*egapesen*] the church and gave himself up for her." Although stated differently so as not to offend outsiders, this is the same encouragement that was given to the wives. The model for a loving relationship is Christ's love for the church.

Another cultural issue comes up in verse 23: "For the husband is the head of the wife as Christ is the head of the church, his body, of which he is the Savior." Although much is written on the meaning of the word translated "head" (Greek *kephale*), most interpret it as "source" or "ruler." In Greek thought, the mind controls the body, which is where the idea of source comes from. The word means simply the top or the head of anything, but it is also used to refer to the one who is "in charge." The idea of the husband being in charge of the wife is offensive to many modern readers, and those who do not understand the textual and cultural contexts behind this scripture try hard to make this word mean something else. Ephesians 5:32 clearly states that the author is "talking about Christ and the church"—not about the relationship between husband and wife (verse 33). What the author teaches in Ephesians 5:23–30 is that Christ is the head, the one in charge, the source, or the top—however one wants to think about Christ's authority.

To help connect the idea for the original audience, the author relies on a commonly held idea in the first century that the man is the public face of the family. The author is not setting a new hierarchy for families; rather, he's using an illustration they would already understand (the idea of a patriarch) to help them understand Christ's authority. He is not using the authority of Christ over the church to teach how relationship should function between men and women! In the first century, the husband took care of all transactions with the public. This was a group-oriented culture, and the welfare of the group was more important than the desires or needs of an individual, which is extremely different from modern Western society, and that is why Western readers today have so much trouble understanding these passages.

Further, it was an honor/shame culture, which means that honor for the family was exceedingly important. Honor back then could be likened to today's credit rating. The more honor a family had, the more status and access to resources they had. Because the man was the public face of the family, the family's honor centered on him. For children or wives to be disobedient was to bring shame on the family and would lower their honor. The first-century Christians lived in this cultural reality. Therefore, for husbands to submit to their wives was a countercultural suggestion. However, Paul and his followers did not care about status. They were slaves to Christ!

Mutual submission in marriage is the same as the mutual submission of all Christians to one another. They are to be submissive to one another in *agape* love, as Christ submitted himself to the cross. This passage does not teach about headship in the family but simply uses the already existent cultural understanding of man's position in the family to teach about the relationship between Christ and the church.

The Household Rules

Several other passages cite common rules of relationship as found in the patriarchal world of the first century. Scholars generally refer to these as "household rules." They can be found in Colossians 3:18–4:1, Titus 2:1–10, and 1 Peter 3:1–7. We will look at them briefly and consider their purpose and context.

Many scholars recognize the similarities between Colossians and Ephesians. Some think they were written about the same time, and some think Colossians is dependent on Ephesians, but many contemporary scholars think Ephesians was written later by a disciple of Paul, and is therefore dependent on Colossians. For our purposes, it is enough to see that there are many similarities between the two letters. The earliest manuscripts do not have "in Ephesus" as an identification of the epistle's recipients, indicating it was likely sent to several churches. It is also more general in its applications than Colossians.

In Colossians, Paul is refuting some misunderstandings of the gospel. The believers in Colossae appear to have been influenced by Judaizers who were actively following Paul's ministries and teaching converts that they had to become Jews to be complete Christians, following the rules related to festivals and diet. In Colossians 2, Paul emphasizes their freedom in Christ from human rules. The beginning of chapter 3 goes on to encourage the Christians who have died to their "earthly nature" (3:5) to realize they have been "raised with Christ" (v. 1) and must live as holy people who are forgiving and humble (v. 12). He says the Colossian Christians are "called to peace" (v. 15).

The combination of holy and peace indicates that there is disorder in the Colossian church. When Paul uses the term "holy" in his writings, it usually means he is calling for order in the Christian lifestyle. In verse 18, Paul goes directly into household instructions after encouraging them to do "whatever you do . . . all in the name of the Lord Jesus" (v. 17). Here the instructions are much shorter and are given without much explanation. The key to understanding the household instructions in Colossians is the need for order. Paul's greatest concern is that Christians meet the standards for good citizens so the message of the gospel is not tarnished by unacceptable behavior. Remember, this is a group-oriented society, so the needs of the individual are subservient to the needs of the group. In this case, evangelism is the goal of the group, so Paul wants to remind the group members that they shouldn't be doing anything that will cause people to reject their message outright because of how they behave.

The passage in Titus 2 does not have the usual household codes. Instead, the instructions are directed toward older men, older women, young men, and slaves. Here the purpose is clear. They are to be examples of Christlikeness for the sake of the gospel: "so that in every way they will make the teaching about God our Savior attractive" (v. 10). Again, the concern here is for evangelism. The application needs to reflect this goal. When we are applying this scripture to our world today, we need to reflect on the evangelistic application of the passage to our current context.

The last household code does not appear in Paul's letters but has a similar purpose. First Peter 3:1–7 addresses only the relationship between husband and wife. In verse 1, wives are encouraged to submit to their husbands "so that, if any of them do not believe the word, they may be won over without words by the behavior of their wives." Again, the goal is evangelism. These were women who were converting to Christianity whose husbands were not believers. Today there are married Muslim women converting to Christianity who can relate to these passages. They are the evangelistic tool to help bring their unbelieving husbands to Christ. In the first century, as in many Islamic cultures today, women would have no option for survival outside of their marriages. Therefore, we must be clear that these passages are not exhortations for women to discard healthy boundaries or to endure abusive treatment. They are, however, specific instructions to women who find themselves in a place where their lives serve as living testimonies to the transformational work of Jesus Christ.

The household codes were not new instructions for Christians but were intended to remind them to be good citizens so new believers would be attracted to the gospel. Because the purpose is evangelistic in nature—to make the gospel more attractive—these scriptures cannot be taken literally thousands of years later in a culture that otherwise looks nothing like the cultures behind these texts. Instead, we must ask ourselves with respect to the world we live in today: what are the requirements to be good people in our society that will make the gospel attractive to those who don't believe?

1 Corinthians 11: Submission and Headship in Worship

According to 1 Corinthians 11, both men and women pray and prophesy (or preach). The issue here is not whether women can pray or preach in the corporate worship context but whether men and women should pray with their heads covered. Paul talks about the relationships of men, women, and Christ in verse 3 in terms of who is the head of whom—but again, this statement is made in the context of what is culturally appropriate. Finally, in verse 11, Paul clearly declares the interdependence of women and men.

In verse 13, he asks the church community to decide the culturally proper dress for women and men leading worship. Paul seems to lean toward head coverings for women because "the very nature of things" teaches that "if a woman has long hair, it is her glory" (vv. 14, 15). In other words, women were expected to cover their heads in that culture. Women who did not cover their heads were often prostitutes, who also might wear their hair short.

Obviously, "the very nature of things" in our modern Western context does not indicate that Christian women must have long hair, or that they should cover their heads with a veil. Modesty is an important value for Christian women in worship leadership, but what modesty entails changes from one culture to another.

1 Corinthians 14 and 1 Timothy 2: Silence and Authority

First Corinthians 14:33–35 reads, "For God is not a God of disorder but of peace—as in all the congregations of the Lord's people. Women should remain silent in the churches.[4] They are not allowed to speak, but must be in submission, as the law says. If they want to inquire about something, they should ask their own husbands at home; for it is disgraceful for a woman to speak in the church." Context is very important to even begin to understand this passage because, first of all, just three chapters earlier in 1 Corinthians 11, Paul tells us that men and women are praying and prophesying (preaching) in the church!

---

4. The 1984 version of the NIV renders the punctuation of these verses thus: "For God is not a God of disorder but of peace. As in all the congregations of the saints, women should remain silent in the churches." The current NIV translation offers a footnote showing the way the former NIV punctuated these sentences, which implies the ambiguity found in the Greek text.

So which is it? Women praying and prophesying, or women being silent? It cannot be both!

The mystery religions of the first century are the first contextual issue. These were the most common religions of the day, called "mystery" because they involved secret ceremonies. Women were prominent in mystery religions, whose rituals usually took place in homes. The purpose of the mystery religions' worship was to work oneself into a frenzy so that one communed with the god being worshiped. Paintings of these religious services regularly show women with their heads uncovered and their hair in total disarray—as if the women were insane. This kind of out-of-control worship is what concerns Paul. Christian worship was held in a private home and practiced private Communion. Therefore, to outsiders, Christianity often looked like a mystery religion. Wearing the symbol of authority (1 Corinthians 11:2–11) needs to be understood in the context of worship. In Jewish worship, men wore shawls over their heads when they prayed, so here Paul encourages women—who might be otherwise lumped in with frenzied mystery religion practitioners—to pray with their heads covered and behave properly.

In 1 Corinthians 14:34, the Greek says *"the* women," indicating a specific group of women who may be uneducated in Scripture but were used to taking the lead in the pagan mystery religion services. Paul is obviously not against women praying and preaching in worship services (see 11:5), but he is against those preaching—whether men *or* women—who are not instructed in the gospel. Finally, this verse uses the passive voice when talking about silence and submission, indicating a voluntary act. And it is not only for women but also for men, as found in 14:28: "Let him/her be silent in the church and let him/her speak [silently] to himself/herself and to God" (author's translation).

The NIV translates 1 Timothy 2:12 as, "I do not permit a woman to teach," but the Greek actually indicates that "I am not presently permitting a woman to teach" is a better, more accurate translation. In the ancient Ephesian cultural context into which the letter to Timothy was sent, there was no Torah training for women, and it is likely these mature Ephesian women were used to leading pagan temple worship. However, because of their lack of education, they were teaching unorthodox lessons. It is no wonder Paul did not allow these newly converted Ephesian women to teach! He would not have allowed uneducated men to teach either. What Paul commands here is highly countercultural, in fact. He commands that the women be taught the Torah! They are to learn in silence, just as the men did.

The phrase "or to assume authority over a man" in this same verse is interesting in literary and contextual ways. The Greek uses the unusual word *authentein*, which is found only here in the New Testament and is translated in literature outside the New Testament as "to domineer, lord it over."[5] As with many words, the meaning changed over time, so it is difficult to know which meaning Paul meant. Catherine Kroeger finds in the ancient texts that this word took on sexual tones and suggests a different contextual understanding: "'I forbid a woman to teach or engage in fertility practices with a man' would imply that the woman should not involve a man in the heretical kind of Christianity which taught licentious behavior as one of its doctrines. Such a female heretic did indeed 'teach to fornicate' in the Thyatiran church mentioned in Revelation 2:20 (cf. 2:14f.;

---

5. Timothy Friberg, Barbara Friberg, and Neva F. Miller, *Analytical Lexicon of the Greek New Testament* (Victoria, BC, Canada: Trafford Publishing, 2005).

Num. 25:3; 31:15f.)."[6] The usual word for "authority" (*exousia*) does not have these connotations, and is used in reference to Christian leadership. The problem of sexual immorality was much more prevalent than we can imagine. In the 1 Timothy passages we see again the call for women to dress modestly and to be decent and proper. The chapter also closes with a strange comment that women will be saved "through childbearing."[7] The point is that we do not know for sure what Paul intended when he used *authentein*. We cannot use this extremely cloudy chapter to counter all the other passages where Paul clearly affirms women in ministry leadership.

Conclusion

Jesus Christ came to bring restoration to creation damaged by human sin. He challenged the sinful order and taught what God originally had in mind. Paul communicates that vision in Galatians 3:28: "There is neither Jew nor Gentile, neither slave nor free, nor is there male and female, for you are all one in Christ Jesus." He advocates mutual submission of all believers and the importance of the use of each one's gifts to build up the body of Christ. The proof-texts we have carefully discussed, when understood in their literary and cultural-historical contexts, also affirm Paul's vision. His emphasis on the importance of evangelism and his concern with the communication of the true gospel have him correcting practices and limiting the preaching or teaching of those who are not educated in the gospel or who lead immoral lives. These admonitions, when understood in context, are not specifically gendered. The early

---

6. Catherine C. Kroeger, "Ancient Heresies and a Strange Greek Verb," *God's Word to Women*, n.d., https://godswordtowomen.org/kroeger_ancient_heresies.htm.

7. See the Kroeger article for more on children born through ritual prostitution as it relates to this statement.

church began the process of working out Jesus's and Paul's vision and its implications for all ethnicities, social statuses, and genders. We are to continue working out this principle of mutual submission and the proclamation of the gospel for all.

Five

Wisdom from the Old Testament

Rev. Dr. Sarah Coleson Derck
Minister and Professor
United States

Many readers of the Bible could rattle off the names of women whose stories are well known from the Old Testament: Sarah, Rachel and Leah, Hannah, Ruth, and Esther. These women are most familiar to us as mothers or wives, but any reader who concluded that Old Testament women were honored *only* for their work as mothers or wives would be misinformed. Old Testament women were active in public leadership in both civic and religious spheres, even if men were more prominent, and even if modern readers have been taught not to notice these women. Many passages testify to the rightness of women sharing in the leadership of God's people alongside their brothers, husbands, fathers, and sons. This chapter will focus first on the created design for all women's leadership in the world, from Genesis 1–3. Then we will consider the women whose stories reveal their own leadership in the community of Israel. Finally, we will explore those passages that teach us, almost in passing, to expect women to lead and minister to God's people.

In the Beginning

Any consideration of women in the Old Testament must begin with its first chapters. Genesis 1:1–2:3 crowns physical creation with the making of humans:

> Then God said, "Let us make humankind in our image, according to our likeness; and let them have dominion over the fish of the sea, and over the birds of the air, and over the cattle, and over all the wild animals of the earth, and over every creeping thing that creeps upon the earth." So God created humankind in his image, in the image of God he created them; male and female he created them. God blessed them, and God said to them, "Be fruitful and multiply, and fill the earth and subdue it; and have dominion over the fish of the sea and over the birds of the air and over every living thing that moves upon the earth."
> (1:26–28, NRSV)

It is helpful to notice that both genders are named explicitly in this context of dominion-giving and commissioning. Unless by willful ignorance, no one could read these verses and conclude that *only men* are in charge. Both male and female humans are image bearers—a metaphor taken from the religious milieux of the ancient Near East, where a deity's image (usually a carved, cast, or sculpted idol) *was* his or her embodied presence in a temple. Both women and men thus carry God's presence into whatever corner of creation they enter.

Both male and female humans are blessed by God, and blessing in the Old Testament usually results in responsibilities for the blessed to assume. Both women and men are charged with procreating; with exploring, settling, and populating the planet; with governing the other creatures; and with causing all creation to flourish. This shared leadership over creation is even more apparent in the Hebrew text, where every pronoun and command takes the plural form. The immediate context of the passage—with its delineation of "humankind" as both "male and female"—insists that the Hebrew forms of "be fruitful," "multiply," "fill," "subdue," and "have dominion," are all plainly directed toward both male and female humans: "y'all be fruitful," "y'all subdue," "y'all have dominion."[1] The Hebrew will not allow us to read these commands as addressing only the first male, or only men in perpetuity. The commission that sets humanity over the rest of creation is given to both male and female humans.

The Eden scene reinforces this shared leadership of creation with a more localized drama (2:4–3:24). The story arc of Eden highlights the reality that the human task of dominion *cannot be completed* only by men. The first human had a task even before being created: to tend the rest of creation. In 2:5, there is no vegetation yet because two prerequisites are lacking: God has not sent any rain yet, and "there was no one to till the ground" (NRSV). The function of humanity is repeated in verse 15, when the first human is placed in the newly made garden "to till it and keep it" (NRSV). Some might argue this work of tilling and keeping was given only to the man, since the woman didn't exist yet. However, as the story unfolds, it becomes clear that a partner is needed for the work: "It is not good that the human should be alone; I will make for him a power facing him as equal" (v. 18, author's translation).[2]

---

1. Author's colloquial translation.

2. "Power facing him as equal" is a translation of the Hebrew phrase *'ezer cenegdo,* based on the work of Joseph E. Coleson, *'Ezer Cenegdo: A Power Like Him, Facing Him as Equal* (Mechanicsburg, PA: Messiah College, 1996), and

The parade of animals (2:19–20) shows the human that no animal is a sufficient partner. We usually read the making of the first woman, and her joining together as one flesh with the first man, in terms of the goodness of marital intimacy. That interpretation is likely part of the point, but all the *actions* that humans perform in Eden concern the physical creation: naming animals, tending the garden, harvesting fruit, making clothes out of leaves. The first pair become a pair precisely so that both can exercise stewardship over Eden.

Even the pair's conversation with the serpent demonstrates this shared task (3:1–4). The responsibilities for the garden ("to till it and keep it" [2:15, NRSV]) and the attending restriction ("freely eat of every tree . . . [except] the tree of the knowledge of good and evil" [2:16, 17, NRSV]) clearly have been shared with the woman, even if they are spoken originally to the man. The woman knows the commands and owns them as her own, and the man does not interject to correct, instruct, or speak for her. Since the responsibility of tending the garden is shared, so too is their abdication of that responsibility. Any orchard keeper knows one cannot take care of a tree without touching it, but the humans seem to have added something to God's original restriction of not eating from it: "nor shall you touch it" (3:3, NRSV). Both choose to eat from the tree they have neglected to tend or even touch, so both share the immediate effects: both have their eyes opened, know their nakedness, make coverings, and hide from God. There is absolutely no hint of hierarchy in Eden until the consequences of sin are imposed in 3:16. Before the fall, only shared responsibility and mutuality in leadership over creation define human relationships.

R. David Freedman, "Woman, a Power Equal to Man," *Biblical Archaeology Review* 9:1 (January/February, 1983), 56–58.

Women Leaders after Eden

Though Eurocentric Christianity has not paid them much attention, many of Eve's female descendants recovered the authority and leadership lost to women in the fall, even before the ministry of the Son began to restore the breaches between men and women, and before the Holy Spirit was poured out upon all followers. Among other roles, women served as prophets, judges (implying also clan leadership and elder status), and queens.

Before we consider their stories, it might be helpful to address one obvious instance of the exclusion of women. Just about the only prominent role women do not inhabit in the Old Testament is priest, which the more patriarchal streams of Christianity have often read as proof that God did not intend women for public ministry. However, several factors must be considered.

First, a specific prohibition against women priests is nowhere to be found in the Old Testament. Even as the priesthood is inaugurated and Aaron and his sons are ordained, there is no explanation for why only the male lineage is chosen (Exodus 28–29; Leviticus 8–10). Readers might wonder why, especially given that Israel's neighbors are perfectly familiar with female priesthood. If no polemic against female priesthood is called for, even given the feminine elements of the Canaanite religions Israel will encounter, maybe the sons are chosen for reasons other than to establish a gender hierarchy in religious service.

Leviticus itself provides pragmatic reasons for the exclusion of women from priestly service in the restricted sections of the tabernacle/temple. The section immediately following the priestly inauguration is often called the Priestly Code (chapters 11–16), and tells priests how to address encounters with blood, disease, corpses, and other situations that render worshipers ceremonially unclean. Among other regulations, the rites for purification of women after childbirth (chapter 13) and during menstruation (chapter 15) are explained. In the normal course of things, an Israelite woman's menstruation and childbearing would render her ritually unclean on a regular basis, therefore making her ineligible for entrance into the sanctuary for several months out of every year. This consideration doesn't even take into account the needs of breastfeeding children, who would keep a woman too busy to serve the worshiping public for weeks away from home. Including Israelite women in the priestly rosters of Yahweh's sanctuary, then, would be completely impractical. This is why female priests in neighboring nations are either celibate or infertile—or regularly abort their pregnancies.

Women Prophets and a Judge

The concern for ritual purity did not keep women out of other spiritually authoritative roles. Several women in the Old Testament are called prophets. The first is Miriam. Though Christian curriculum usually focuses on her childhood care for baby Moses, subsequent texts preserve a robust legacy for her. Miriam is never called a wife or mother, but she is named a prophet in Exodus 15:20—the first woman designated as such. She leads the congregation in worship right after the miraculous sea crossing (vv. 20–21); Jewish tradition even holds that the song in verses 1–18, which Miriam leads the women in singing again a few verses later, is actually her own composition. Her opposition to Moses's non-Israelite wife in Numbers 12 is significant precisely because Miriam occupies a position of authority and influence. This understanding of her work is reflected in the prophet Micah, who remembers Miriam as co-leader of the exodus right alongside her brothers (6:4). Such reverence for Miriam's leadership in Israel helps explain why the New Testament attests to no fewer than seven Jewish women named

Mary (the Hebrew name "Miriam" is usually rendered "Maria" in Greek).[3] She is a worthy namesake, indeed.

Deborah, too, was a prophet, but she was also a judge. As her story unfolds in Judges 4–5, a picture emerges of the great authority and influence she wields. It is commonly argued that the judges in the book of Judges were not actual legal agents but leaders who judged Israel's enemies through military defeat. Deborah's story does not align with that argument. Deborah occupies a seat of judgment for all Israel that is so well established that the palm tree under which she hears cases is called by her own name (Judges 4:4–5). Since she is called a prophet and a judge, Deborah probably entertains requests for both spiritual guidance and legal mediation.

Deborah is the only woman we know of to ever be called a judge, but those who claim this as evidence that she was the only woman ever to serve would do well to notice that the narrator feels no need to comment on or explain her status to readers. Her leadership is accepted by all Israel, which suggests she was not alone as a female judge. Judges were usually chosen from among the elders of a clan and tribe, so it is a reasonable supposition that Deborah and her husband, Lappidoth, are prominent leaders of the community. But Deborah, not Lappidoth, judges and prophesies.

As a prophet, Deborah hears the word of the Lord and does not hesitate to pass it along to others. She wields enough influence to summon one of Israel's other leaders, the general Barak, and to command him into battle (4:6). Deborah does not sit back under the shade of her tree and wait for the battle report. Instead, she joins Barak at the front of the column of ten thousand soldiers, going right into battle (vv. 9–10). Her leadership

---

3. See entries "Mary 1" through "Mary 7" in Meyers, et. al., *Women in Scripture*, 116–24.

is spiritual, legal, and military, and it earns Deborah the title "mother in Israel" (5:7).

Huldah's story is not long or elaborate, and we know next to nothing about her, except that she was a Jerusalem prophet in the era of the divided monarchy, and she was married to the keeper of the royal wardrobe (2 Kings 22:14–20; 2 Chronicles 34:11–28). When King Josiah's workmen find the book of the Law in the long-neglected temple, Huldah is consulted for a word from the Lord regarding the consequences for the nation's neglect of God. She delivers an oracle of judgment upon the nation while holding out hope for Josiah's own life and legacy due to his campaign of reform. In the process, she validates a text as Scripture, "the first recognizable act in the long process of canon formation."[4]

Huldah is an obscure figure, but she is notable for several reasons. She is one of the few women whose stories from the first history of the monarchy (Samuel–Kings) are included in full in the second history (Chronicles): Hannah, Abigail, Tamar, Bathsheba, Milcah, and many others are either left out or mentioned only in passing by the Chronicler. She is also one of only three women who speak in Chronicles (the other two are the queen of Sheba and Queen Athaliah). Huldah's work was seen as worthy of preservation in the task of telling and retelling the history of God and Israel. Perhaps most importantly, her prophetic position in such a time of national tumult and reform testifies to the ongoing work of God through women in Israel.

Two other female prophets are mentioned in the Old Testament. Noadiah was a prophet during the rebuilding of Jerusalem after the exile. Her opposition to Nehemiah wields such influence that she nearly succeeds in intimidating him (Nehe-

---

4. Claudia Van Camp, "Huldah," *Women in Scripture*, 96.

miah 6:14). Isaiah's own wife is called a prophet too (Isaiah 8:3–4), and although the narrative does not include her name or any of her more typical prophetic activity, she does perform a prophetic sign-act by bearing in her own body the sign of God's judgment—the child Maher-shalal-hash-baz.

Two other women leaders deserve consideration: local wise women who led during the reign of David. "Wise woman" is a cognate term with "prophet;" wise women and wise men tended to employ human wisdom and subtle skill in negotiation rather than prophetic oracles, though this distinction is neither absolute nor universal. The religious activity of these two wise women is not in the public worship center or even local shrines but in the realm of diplomacy, urging the king toward more righteous choices. The wise woman of Tekoa (2 Samuel 14:1–20) is the female counterpart of Nathan the prophet. Where Nathan confronts David over his sin against Bathsheba and Uriah (2 Samuel 12), the wise woman of Tekoa challenges David's neglect of the breach with his son Absalom, who avenges the rape of Tamar. The wise woman of Abel of Beth-maacah stops a siege and saves her walled town from destruction when David's general Joab is pursuing a traitor (2 Samuel 20:14–22). Both wise women exercise unambiguous authority that is accepted without question.

Queens

Easily the most famous queen in the Old Testament, Esther is worthy of our admiration because of her leadership on behalf of the entire community of Jews living in the Persian realm. She uses her royal power to establish not only the safety of her people but also a new holy festival. As she prepares to fight against Haman's genocidal decree, Esther commands a three-day fast for all the Jews in the capital city of Susa (Esther 4:16). It was Mordecai's idea for Esther to approach the king uninvited, but it is Esther's idea to call the people to prayer and fasting in preparation. It is worth noting that Mordecai responds with immediate obedience to his young relative: he "went away and did everything as Esther had ordered him" (4:17, NRSV). This verse marks a stark transition from Esther being ordered and directed by everyone else to her own ideas and commands beginning to drive the action. She sets up Mordecai as Haman's replacement (8:1-2). She arranges for the defense of the Jewish people against Haman's planned attacks (8:7, 12-13). Finally, she inaugurates the feast of Purim to commemorate God's protection of the Persian Jews, and Purim is still observed today (8:24-32).

Two other queens in Israel exercise great power: Jezebel (1 Kings 16-21; 2 Kings 9) and Athaliah (2 Kings 11). Both are infamous for their wickedness, and they do not provide worthy examples for the leadership of women in the church today. However, their very existence as queens with real political power refutes the idea that women in Israel had no role in public life. Theologically speaking it was their wickedness—not their gender—that was problematic in their leadership roles.

Israelite society made room for women in almost every position of influence and authority. When compared to their male colleagues, women appear to be rare in the biblical story arc, leading some to think they are the exception to a perceived rule of male leadership. However, the next section will add to the evidence that this perception is an accident of literary processes, rather than the complete picture of reality in Israel.

Other Leaders

Across the pages of the Old Testament, women exercise leadership in every sphere of human life. The legal texts of the Pentateuch focus the reader's attention on the space and personnel of the public sanctuary (the tabernacle), and the monarchical histories concentrate on the palace and temple realms (1 Samuel-2 Chronicles). Unfortunately for our purposes, these emphases obscure the reality that, for the vast majority of Israelites, the religion of Israel was a domestic one, with the bulk of worship occurring at home within the family. We should not be surprised to notice, then, at least as a starting point, that women are intentionally mentioned as members of the covenant community (e.g., Deuteronomy 12:12; 16:11, 14), and are noted as attending services and offering sacrifices in multiple passages.

In the household context, women partner with their male family members in the growth or husbandry and preparation of vegetable and animal sacrifices. They pray and sing together in weekly Sabbath and monthly New Moon worship, make pilgrimage for major festivals, and observe the law together as a family unit. Women can make their own vows (1 Samuel 1–3) and even become Nazirites (Numbers 6:2). The mother's teaching of the law to her children is expected to provide a lifelong standard for wisdom and righteousness (Proverbs 1:8–9; 6:20–22; 31:1–9).

More than just participation, however, some passages testify to the leadership of women in Israelite life and worship. These can be divided into the basic categories of religious celebrants and secular professionals (though that distinction would make no sense in the ancient Near East). As we have seen before, some of these women emerge more clearly in the Hebrew text than in English translation. Sometimes this is due to Hebrew feminine endings that do not always get translated into English; sometimes it is simply not apparent in English that a personal name is actually a woman's.

There is ample evidence of women who operated as guild professionals and leaders in many trades of ancient Israel. Female textile artists contributed their skills to the furnishing of the tabernacle (Exodus 35:25–26). Women in the early monarchy made careers for themselves as royal perfumers, cooks, and bakers (1 Samuel 8:13). Ezra 2:55 and Nehemiah 7:57 list Hassophereth/Sophereth as one of Solomon's servants, whose descendants are counted among those returning from exile. This personal name literally means "female scribe," indicating that Solomon employed a woman for his scribe, which was a position that required intensive education and the king's confidence. This scribe was prominent enough that, centuries later, her descendants warrant naming among the returnees.

Other women are notable for their command of wealth and building power. One woman, Sheerah, was a wealthy entrepreneur who built three towns (1 Chronicles 7:24). A whole family of female builders is named among the rebuilders of Jerusalem: the daughters of Shallum, who literally helped rebuild the walls (Nehemiah 3:12). The "Shunammite woman" (2 Kings 4:8–37; 8:1–6) is a wealthy landowner who commands servants, commissions a building project, moves her household in the face of a famine, and appeals to the king for the return of her land rights.

Women also serve as religious authorities and leaders. Female musicians are regular features in Israel's victory celebrations (Exodus 15:20–21; 1 Samuel 18:6–7; Judges 11:34; Jeremiah 31:4, 13)—singing, dancing, and playing frame drums ("tambourines" is an anachronistic translation).[5] These women drummers feature in religious processions (Psalm 68:25); female singers perform in palace and religious ceremonies as well as private feasts and celebrations (2 Samuel 19:35; Ecclesiastes 2:8; Ezra 2:65; Nehemiah 7:67). Sometimes these women musicians serve also as professional mourners (2 Chronicles 35:25; Jeremiah 9:17–20; Ezekiel 32:16).

---

5. Carol Meyers, "Women with Hand-Drums, Dancing," *Women in Scripture*, 190.

Several texts indicate more explicit ministry leadership among the women of Israel. Though rarely acknowledged in Christian teaching and preaching, women are not entirely excluded from service at the sanctuary. Indeed, women minister at the entrance to the tent of meeting, or tabernacle (Exodus 38:8; 1 Samuel 2:22). No description of their service is provided, but their role is likely something to do with helping worshipers prepare to enter the holy space, or prepare their sacrifices. There is no indication these women minister only among women worshipers.

Two poetic passages assume that those who herald the good news of God will include women proclaimers. Psalm 68:11 commends the women heralds who proclaim the victorious God: "Yahweh gives the command; the women heralds are a great army" (author's translation).[6] Isaiah 40:9 commands female heralds to proclaim the arrival of God to Zion, using the feminine form only here and in Psalm 68:11. To get the point across in English, we would have to employ something like the awkward term "heraldress": "Get yourself up to a high mountain, heraldress of good tidings to Zion; lift up your voice with strength, heraldress of good tidings to Jerusalem; rise, woman, and do not fear! Say to the cities of Judah, 'Here is your God!'" (author's translation).

Finally, the prophet Joel foresees a day when the women we have considered here will be joined in ministry by all their sisters (Joel 2:28–29). Joel employs a series of three *merisms* to describe the universal gift of the Spirit. A merism is a pair of nouns that represent two opposites and are intended to include everything between the two extremes—for example, "from New York to L. A." or "from north to south." When the Spirit is

---

6. Even though the Hebrew uses feminine language, the NRSV does not make the gender distinction clear outside of a footnote. The NIV says "the women who proclaim it."

given to all, Joel says, all Israel's daughters will join their brothers as prophets. Both sons and daughters will proclaim oracles. Both old people and young people will experience prophetic dreams and visions (the insertion of "men" into many modern translations ignores the gender-inclusive use of the masculine plural in Hebrew). Both male and female slaves will join the community as full participants in the Spirit.

Final Thoughts

A closer look at the complete corpus of the Old Testament has revealed a much more robust picture of the ministry and authority of women in Israel than is usually credited. From her role as co-regent over all creation to prophetic and sanctuary ministry, from professional skills to political power to family leadership, woman is a regular partner in the work of God among the people of God. The Old Testament casts a vision of mutual leadership in Eden, then includes dozens of instances of women reclaiming this leadership and, in doing so, sets the stage for its final restoration through the work of the Son and the Holy Spirit.

Six

Challenges and Blessings of Church Planting

Rev. Selena Freeman
Minister and Church Planter
United States

It was my first district ministry retreat as a church planter. The Well Church was brand new, and I was excited to be invited to the retreat. I sat with my husband on one side of me and twenty-three-year-old Dylan, the other co-lead pastor of The Well, on the other. As we anticipated the upcoming meal and speaker, a kind pastor from our district approached our table with a big smile. He extended his hand to my husband and said, "I am hearing wonderful things about this new church plant of yours! Let's have coffee sometime soon!" The pastor's intentions were pure in trying to encourage us, but he automatically assumed that the forty-year-old man at the table must be the pastor of this new church. After all, Dylan looked like a kid, and I was a woman. During the retreat, we had the opportunity to correct this pastor and explain that Dylan and I were co-pastors of The

Well and that my husband was a house contractor and not a pastor at all. He was apologetic, and offered to take Dylan for coffee. As a church planter and pastor who is also a woman, I have experienced incredible challenges and blessings. I hope you'll find encouragement from my sharing a few of them.

Ordinary Obedience and Destiny Moments

Ordinary obedience and destiny moments may not sound like they go together, but they do. In my life, they always have. Often, our Father works by allowing what we see in the natural and what he does in the supernatural to collide—allowing "everyday" and "once in a lifetime" to meet, and ordinary and extraordinary to become one.

I was called into ministry as a twelve-year-old at church camp. I had never seen a female pastor or even heard a woman preach, so I assumed I would marry a pastor or become a missionary. I would go on to marry Jon, an incredible man who became a homebuilder, and I became a high school speech and theater teacher who took several years off to be a stay-at-home mom. During this time, Jon and I volunteered as youth leaders in a small Nazarene church. Life was good; however, after our second child was born, I experienced intense depression and began to question my life as a whole. During this crisis experience, I fully surrendered my will to God's and was sanctified— truly set apart for God's use. He brought me back to his call of ministry upon my life. Having completed a bachelor's degree in education and a master's degree in counseling, I began my ministry classes at age twenty-nine. I spent the next six years volunteering in youth ministry, raising my children, and completing the ministry preparation process. It was a grind, but God was preparing me for his promise.

I was hired as a staff member at the church where I had volunteered for years, I completed ordination, and I spent the next twelve years as a youth pastor. Some of the greatest memories and proudest moments in my calling have come from those eighteen years in youth ministry. During those years, Jon and I had many teens pass through our home. One of those teens was Dylan Robinson. We met Dylan when he was a broken, sixteen-year-old drug addict living between his grandparents' home and friends' homes because both parents were basically on the street. Through a crazy course of events, Dylan came to live with our family and became a forever part of our family as our godson.

Mark Bane also came into our lives during this time. This new district superintendent was unlike anyone I had met before: he *saw* me. Mark invited Jon and me to a church-planting assessment. I had no idea what it was but was happy to be invited, so I jumped at the chance. As the assessment drew closer, I realized it was a big deal. We were asked to submit photos, do personality tests, and answer a lot of questions. I filled everything out for both of us to keep Jon from backing out. At the assessment, Jon saw our photos and profiles and asked, "What exactly are we doing here?" I honestly told him that I truly had no idea! I had no desire to plant a church, nor did I have any understanding of what it really meant. At the end of the weekend, the assessors told us we were approved to plant a church. *What?! What does that mean?* We had powered through the interesting experience with no intention of ever planting a church.

Life went on, and I was convinced I would continue in youth ministry well into my sixties. One day, a young lady I had mentored came to me to express her desire to begin the journey toward pastoral ministry. I set up a meeting for us with Mark Bane, since he had been so encouraging to me. As Mark got to hear Jeni share her hopes and aspirations for the future, he looked across the table and said, "What about you, Selena?" I responded that God had called me to youth ministry in Marsh-field, Missouri.

That day would become one of those collisions of ordinary obedience and destiny moments. I did not think about it until a couple days later. I was cleaning my house, fully immersed in the ordinary tasks of everyday life. To be specific, I was Swiffer-ing my floors, which I love to do. I was behind my couch to get the dust hiding there when the Spirit of the living God literally stopped me in my tracks. A gentle whisper in my soul brought me to my knees, and the Lord confirmed that I needed to listen to what he was saying to me through Mark. I called Mark that very day to share what had happened, we set up a meeting the next week, and our journey toward planting The Well began.

One of the things I have learned in the years of church planting is that our destiny is designed in the details. God brings about the things that only God can as we simply obey him in what seem like the ordinary acts of everyday life. One of my favorite Mark Batterson quotes is: "God is great not just because nothing is too big for him. God is great because nothing is too small for him either."[1] What are the small acts of obedience that God is calling you to today that may change your tomorrow?

The Vision Isn't Yours, and Neither Is the Church

Over the next few months, our family began to attend train-ing sessions on church planting, and we learned many things. First and foremost, we had to figure out the vision and mission for the church we would plant.

When Dylan first came to our home, our only goals were to introduce him to Christ and get him through high school. As

---

1. Mark Batterson, *In a Pit with a Lion on a Snowy Day: How to Survive and Thrive When Opportunity Roars* (Colorado Springs: Multnomah, 2006).

a junior, he had been absent more days of high school than he had been present. During his senior year in 2015, he had the opportunity to attend the Nazarene Youth Conference (NYC) in Louisville, Kentucky, with our youth group. While Francis Chan spoke at NYC, God called Dylan into ministry. Not only did Dylan graduate from high school, but he also graduated from college, became a youth pastor, and helped plant The Well.

We spent hours praying and planning, thinking God might want us to start a coffee shop. I mean, did he really call us to plant a church? What should it look like? Where should it be? What should we call it? Whom should we reach? How would we pay for it? We soon realized we had to hear again from God, and we couldn't take another step until we did. The vision was not something we could create but something we had to discern. With our Bibles and Mark Batterson's book *The Circle Maker* in hand, we continued to pray and fast until God allowed us to see his vision for The Well.

One of my favorite authors, Jentezen Franklin, offers great wisdom on vision. He says, "There is a difference between 'vision' and 'ambition.' Vision comes from God, and it will help people. Ambition comes from your flesh, and it will help you use people. A lot of people try to legitimize ambition for vision, but there is a big difference. Vision is when God gives it, and it is about helping other people."[2]

Church planting could not be a means to fulfill my ambition but had to be the result of receiving God's vision. If you plant *your* church, it will be just that—yours—and the power, presence, and favor of God will not be there. People come to me regularly, men *and* women, to talk about church planting

---

2. Jentezen Franklin, *The Jentezen Franklin Legacy Bible* (Austin, TX: Fedd Books, 2018), 1131.

with well-thought-out vision and mission statements, great plans, and also hearts full of pride, hurt, and ambition. I see it and recognize it because I have been there. I get it, and you must get rid of it—because the church isn't yours, and neither is the vision.

What about My Kids?

Church planting is not a new job or a career shift; it is a total life change. When God called us to plant The Well, our kids were fifteen and twelve, and had been in the same church in the same town with our entire family since birth. Our kids had literally been raised in the youth group and were finally old enough to actually *be* in the youth group, but now Jon and I were transitioning them into a completely new way of life. Of all the things that brought me pause in this journey, the impact that it would have on our kids was one of the greatest. Kaden and Krenna had just spent the last five years of their lives sharing our home with Dylan and hundreds of other teens—and now we were asking them to leave the church they loved.

All I can say is that God is good and so faithful! Over our first three years at The Well, I watched God develop crazy faith in the lives of our kids. I watched them develop a love for and dependence on God that I am not sure they would have developed had we not taken this step of faith as a family. I watched them explore their own gifts and callings to become leaders in the church and among their peers.

Knowing my reservations about the impact planting a church would have on our kids, God used them in a couple of my most affirming moments during this time. Early on, God gave me Revelation 3:8: "I know your deeds. See, I have placed before you an open door that no one can shut. I know that you have little strength, yet you have kept my word and have not denied my name." In the course of a month, that verse had already shown up in my daily reading, in a sermon I heard, and at a conference I attended.

One day, I drove Krenna to school, having been up most of the night running scenarios of success and failure through my mind and still uncertain what we were supposed to do. Sitting in the school's drop-off line, my twelve-year-old daughter shared with me that the Lord told her I was supposed to read Revelation 3:8. *Wait, what?!* I would love to tell you that our family is just so supernaturally in tune that it was common for me to receive revelation from my child, but she had never done anything like that before. As she hopped out of the car that morning with her backpack and lunchbox in hand and bounced into school in her Krenna way, I was in shock as tears streamed down my face with the reassurance that God would not only take care of my baby girl in all this but also that it was what he had for her life.

Okay, God, but what about Kaden? Krenna was always up for adventure, but Kaden was more reserved and did not like change. We had already stretched him beyond his comfort zone by asking him to welcome Dylan, a former drug addict, into our home. What would be the impact of this new adventure on him?

One night, our family and a few friends were gathered in our home, talking and vision-casting for the future church. God had given us The Well's name through John 4, where Jesus speaks with and ministers to the woman at the well, and confirmed it through a young man in our youth group. So that night, we looked at the story in John 4, brainstorming words we could use in our mission statement that were rooted in that narrative. It was clear that God had *found* the woman where she was in her everyday life. After Jesus found her, he told her of the life-giving water he had to offer. He told her she could be *filled* and never thirst again.

We had two words, but we wanted three. What would our last word be? A group of us continued to discuss the story as fifteen-year-old Kaden sat on the couch. I am not sure I was aware he was paying any attention to the conversation. Suddenly Kaden yelled out, "Freed! God *freed* her to go and tell others about him!" Yes—she was found, filled, and freed! The Well would be "a church where all people could be found by the grace of God, filled by the power of the Holy Spirit, and freed to love like Christ."

When God calls you, he also calls your family! God used our kids to affirm our assignment every step of the way. He also used our assignment to affirm our kids and grow them into the young adults he was creating them to be. I am not suggesting it has not been hard at times, but as you allow your kids to be part of the process of planting, you will teach them to discern the Father's vision for their lives as well. You can trust our Father with your kids.

Power in the Process

There are several models of church plants, but I knew early on that God had called us to build a team. Frances Frei and Anne Morriss say that leadership isn't about the work you do; it is about the work that you unleash others to do.[3] I had no desire to be a one-woman show. The church we had been part of for eighteen years graciously allowed us to build a team from the congregation. Twenty-eight multigenerational leaders committed to plant The Well in a larger town about thirty miles away. Everyone in this group would have a role.

I am not much of a football fan, but one of my favorite one-liners comes from *Remember the Titans*, a football movie

---

3. Frances Frei and Anne Morriss, *Unleashed: The Unapologetic Leader's Guide to Empowering Everyone around You* (Boston: Harvard Business Review Press, 2020).

where the coach teaches that "attitude reflects leadership." If you are a leader, reflect long and hard on that. If you don't like your team or your team's attitude, look no further than yourself. Another favorite quote that many different people have said is, "You can teach what you know, but you reproduce who you are." When God called me to plant a church, he called me to empower people and raise up leaders in the power and presence of his Holy Spirit. God clearly gave me four core values for myself and the church:

- PRAYER—we will do nothing without it;
- PEOPLE—they must be the reason for everything we do;
- PASSION—we will give our lives to this;
- PROCESS—if it is worth doing, it is worth doing right.

For six months we prayed, prepared, and practiced the process of planting a new church. We met in a small movie theater, an apartment complex, and a rural campground in the middle of nowhere. There were no social media posts, invite cards, or promotional events. We worshiped, preached, prayed, served, prepared, and walked through a process. We created our culture and DNA. We lived out the core values. Those six months were crucial in the life of The Well. Now, years later, we have a process of discipleship, a process of multiplication, and a process of ordination with numerous men and women walking it out, along with staff, team leaders, hundreds of volunteers, and new church planters. There is power in the process through the presence of the Holy Spirit.

Ministry Is a Marathon

One of the most wonderful—yet terrible—things about church planting is that things are always changing. It is wonderful in that there is freedom to try new things, go new places, and challenge people in new ways. It is terrible because it can feel as though you are trying to drink water from a fire hose. In fact, for the first year of our planting journey, I felt like I was going to throw up every single day. I was in a constant state of fear and exhaustion. When it comes to work ethic, my husband would lovingly describe me as a "grinder." I have often felt pride in that description, but if I am not careful, I will grind myself and everyone around me right into the ground.

The first couple years of our church plant were absolutely amazing as we saw God's incredible work, but I was on the verge of total burnout. The church was growing, yet I was shrinking. I was sleeping a few hours a night while neglecting my marriage, my family, and myself. I joke that I gained more weight helping birth a church than I did giving birth to two children. With no office or permanent building that first year, I spent hours at Panera Bread. It may be clean food, but eating there multiple times each day and not allowing time for exercise or sleep will catch up with you! That is an embarrassing picture to paint of myself, but it is true, and it reflects an obstacle church planters must figure out how to overcome.

An incredible pastor and mentor reminded me that ministry is a marathon, not a sprint. I now understand that our days and weeks may not be perfectly balanced, but our *seasons* must be. A season of extreme work must be followed by a season of rest. A season of vision and growth must be followed by a season of reflection. If we are in this for the long haul, we must find rhythm and rest along the way.

Holding On and Letting Go

After our pre-launch season, The Well officially launched in a hotel ballroom that would hold about three hundred people. It was a great space, and the hotel was wonderful to work with. For the first year, we set up and tore down each Sunday. Our body had grown to about two hundred, and the ballroom was not cheap, so it was time to look for a more permanent location. God led us to a location that was being revitalized in the heart of downtown Springfield, Missouri. There was no way we could afford the space, but God did what God does, and we moved on our first birthday. Although the space was fantastic and it was ours, it was not large. It seated 240 people, and within a few months, we had gone to three Sunday morning services and had added a Friday night recovery service. We did not want to move but knew we had to consider a second location for space and impact. We found a church for sale, five miles away and on the north side of town, which had been our heart all along. This property was also out of our price range, but God provided again through a capital campaign, and we planted the second campus on our third birthday.

The plan was for me to lead the northside campus, Dylan to lead the downtown campus, and our recovery minister, Brandon Lien, to lead the Friday night ministry. However, God was shifting Dylan's heart toward full-time evangelism. I was still getting to know and trust Brandon; I trusted him with recovery ministry, but I didn't know if his raw, confrontational style would work for Sunday mornings. For the first couple months of the transition, Brandon and I alternated campuses weekly as preaching pastors. It was a mess. People were leaving. We weren't connecting with anyone. We didn't know if we were coming or going. We entertained the idea of a simulcast before it became clear that it wasn't an option that would work for us. In that season, God revealed to me: *Delegate or die! Selena, you are going to kill yourself and the church. You have to let go.* I was more interested in building God's kingdom than mine. I refused to kill the church because of my refusal to shift.

In the first four years of our church-plant journey, we watched God grow a core group of twenty-eight people meeting in my living room, to more than a thousand people meeting across three campuses on a weekly basis. I experienced crippling challenges, but I was also blessed beyond any measure of my imagination. Each step of the way, the Father has continued to speak John 15:16 over my life, which reminds me, "You did not choose me, but I chose you and appointed you so that you might go and bear fruit—fruit that will last—and so that whatever you ask in my name the Father will give you." I pray that you also receive this word today as a promise over your life and calling, and have found encouragement on your journey as I have shared some of mine.

Conclusion

The pages of this book may challenge some of our traditional assumptions regarding the place of women in ministry. When Jesus confronts his followers, a challenge normally ensues. The presence of Jesus can make us uncomfortable—in a good way. Empowered by the Holy Spirit, God's sons and daughters are encouraged to become ministers of the gospel of Jesus Christ.

Seven
Serving God with Joy

Rev. Phumzile Phago
Minister
Republic of South Africa

For we are God's masterpiece. He has created us anew in Christ Jesus,
so we can do the good things he planned for us long ago.
—*Ephesians 2:10, NLT*

Scripture reveals to us how precious we are in the eyes of God; we are God's creative artwork. This truth is not unique to those who serve in ministry, but there is something about answering and responding to the call that reveals God's beautiful and holy creativity. Responding to the call is deeply personal, and comes from the overflow of a relationship with Jesus Christ. We are drawn toward ministry—to answering the call—because we have fallen in love with Jesus Christ. At the same time, the power of God is revealed in us as we are transformed on a daily basis, becoming more like Christ. Wherever we go, we are to reflect Christ in the way we conduct ourselves. Only through the power of God in and through us are we enabled to know God more. This is the beauty of our relationship with God because, as much as God may want us to serve him, he is primarily concerned about the ways in which we are being formed and about who we are becoming in the process.

We Are Saved to Serve

Through salvation we are able to know God and his plan for our lives. When God called me into ministry, it was not easy. As a young girl from a rural area, I did not think I had much to give; therefore, I struggled to accept the call. I felt I could still serve God while living my own life, and I told myself I didn't have to leave everything to do ministry. But I was convicted when I read the Bible, for there I could see Jesus calling his disciples—and they left everything and followed him.

Ministry is costly. You cannot come into this path while still owning your life. You must die to self so that Christ can be alive in you, and you must also allow God to shape you as he directs your path. I wrestled with God, but the day I surrendered, I experienced peace and joy unspeakable. God's presence was overwhelming, and from that day onward I decided that is where I want to be for the rest of my life. My prayer is that I will humbly walk with him daily and finish well until the day I see his face.

For those serving in ministry, there are strategies to follow so that we will all finish well. These points that I share with you are very close to my heart.

Think Generationally

In Genesis, God states clearly the reason he has called Abraham: "For I have chosen him, so that he will direct his children and his household after him to keep the way of the LORD by doing what is right and just, so that the LORD will bring about for Abraham what he has promised him" (18:19). God chose Abraham for two things: (1) to keep the way of the Lord—which demands a relationship. Amos 3:3 says, "Do two walk together unless they have agreed to do so?"; and (2) to teach his children and family to honor God and keep the ways of God by doing what is right. And God says only then will the Lord fulfill what he has promised to Abraham. It's very important to notice this. We are chosen by God for himself. Women in ministry—indeed, everyone who is called to ministry—must understand that the calling is not ours. It is God's call upon our lives. Therefore, the way we handle ourselves will determine the success God will bring our way in ministry.

First and foremost, God is calling us to himself. He is calling us to a lifelong relationship. You cannot keep the way of the Lord unless you have a relationship with God. There is a difference between knowing someone and having an intimate relationship with someone. It is not enough to have knowledge *about* someone. For example, if I meet the author John Maxwell and take a picture with him, and even post the picture on social media, this does not mean I really know him or have a relationship with him. I happen to admire him and know him as a public figure, but I don't have a relationship with him. The same principle applies to our relationship with God. To walk with God and be used by God, we must move from knowing about God to having a relationship with God. Ministry demands a daily, intimate relationship with God. Remember that you are chosen to serve God in your generation. God singled out Abraham to honor him and to teach his children and family to do likewise.

Women in ministry must always remember that they are to serve as nation carriers and nation builders. As servants of God, ministers are to carry the message of reconciliation, hope, re-demption, love, and forgiveness. Never to be forgotten are the messages of healing and restoration. Women of God are preg-nant with something bigger than themselves. God's call upon is not about the individual; it's about the surrounding people and your entire generation.

Remember the story of Mary, the mother of Jesus? Her re-sponse to the call of God was never about her, but it was about God's mission, plan, and purpose for all of humanity. When God looked down on earth, he saw Mary as a vessel he could use to bring about the salvation of the whole world. In God's plan to save humanity, to secure the salvation of all of creation, he stepped in and became human. Beautifully, Mary answered God's call, which changed the future hope of all humankind.

I don't think it was easy for Mary. Her life story shows the highest level of sacrificial love, servanthood, and total surren-der. When the angel of the Lord visited, her response was that of total surrender. It's okay to consider the cost before we jump, but Mary's quick response is amazing, revealing her high level of faith in God. Listen to her beautiful response in Luke 1:38: "Here am I, the servant of the Lord; let it be with me according to your word" (NRSV).

Not many in our era would respond like Mary because, by nature, we want to be in charge of our lives. Control is of ut-most importance, and anything that enters our space that we can't control becomes a threat. In all circumstances we want to calculate the risk and benefits before making a decision. When it comes to ministry, we need to think differently because min-istry requires a heart fully yielded to the will of God. This is the secret of a fulfilled life. We are filled with great joy when our lives are fully aligned to God's will. We are to be filled with humility and be willing to die to self when we receive the call from God. To be called by God or appointed by God for any role, large or small, is an honor and a privilege that should keep us in a continual state of humility before him.

In Mary's story we find lessons for all who are engaged in ministry, and if we are willing to learn, our service in the kingdom of God will be made complete. Trusting God is significant when it comes to ministry. Just like Mary, the call may seem unexpected or unexplainable, but she trusted. Our role is to obey God, and trust that his purposes for our lives are good and perfect. Mary's response to God's plan for humanity was self-sacrifice. For successful ministry, we must develop sensitive ears and responsive hearts toward the whispers of the Holy Spirit. God must have first priority in all we say and do, and we must always be willing to move in the direction God is leading, no matter the season of life. When we move in the direction of God, we will discover great joy.

There is an old hymn that reminds us of the priority of obedience: "Trust and obey, for there's no other way to be happy in Jesus but to trust and obey."[1] For each and every generation, God has appointed those who will fulfill God's mission and purpose. God is not looking for perfect people; he's looking for willing hearts. God knows what he's asking of you and has no expectation for you to follow the call in your own strength. The good news is that when God calls, he also empowers.

One can imagine Mary was full of questions as she thought about facing Joseph with the news the angel brought her. *What will Joseph think about me when he sees me pregnant? If I tell him about my experience, will he believe me? What about his family? What about the community? What will they think of me? How is this going to affect my life, and what will it do to my reputation in the community?* The truth is, if you answer the call to ministry,

---

1. John H. Sammis (words, 1887) and Daniel B. Towner (music, 1887), "Trust and Obey," *Sing to the Lord: Hymnal* (Kansas City, MO: Lillenas Publishing Company, 1993), #437.

you must be ready to suffer persecution, lose your reputation, and suffer rejection. If you are not willing to pay the price, you may as well stay far away. We know that Jesus, the Son of God, suffered, and why should we be any better off? Are you willing to pay the price? If your answer is yes, then welcome to ministry. Mary chose to trust God, and so must we!

We don't know much about the years when Mary was raising her son. In some ways it must have been a blessing and a delight, but it also must have been hard work and joy. In Luke's Gospel we read about Jesus's trip to the temple when he was twelve. Mary and Joseph lose Jesus on that trip, and it is probably not easy for them to understand their child, but they raise him faithfully and with joy (Luke 2:41–52). As hard and challenging as it was, Mary stood firm during pain, doubt, shame and fear. Throughout this entire season, "Mary treasured up all these things and pondered them in her heart" (v. 19).

Mary was also willing to grow in her faith. We find her in the very opening of Jesus's story, at the cross, and later a faithful member of the early Christian church. She was an example of Paul's words to the church in Philippi: "I am confident of this, that the one who began a good work among you will bring it to completion by the day of Jesus Christ" (Philippians 1:6, NRSV). God continued to do his good work in and through Mary. She discovered that God's grace is sufficient for every step of the journey. That same grace is available for all who step up in faith to answer the call to serve the Lord. May we join with Mary responding, "Here am I, the servant of the Lord; let it be with me according to your word" (Luke 1:38, NRSV).

Women in ministry birth leaders, preachers, and strong family-oriented men and women who will be faithful in their marriages and raise up godly children. Without Abraham, Isaac and Jacob could not function. Thinking generationally means no one should be left behind, and ministry must be intentional from the home, to church, to the local community. There must not be a generational gap. All the generations—from Abraham down to the twelve sons of Jacob, and beyond—work together. Abraham's role is to bless and give resources to Isaac. Isaac's role is to receive the resources with humility, not entitlement. Then Isaac releases the blessing and resources to Jacob, who continues the cycle. Jacob should never forget where he came from. With humility and respect for those who have gone before him, Jacob reveres Abraham and Isaac. He honors the leaders and continuously seeks and listens to the advice and wisdom of Abraham and Isaac even as he raises the new generation of sons who will become the twelve tribes of Israel. It is possible for all of these to work together as they pass the baton from one generation to the next. They are able to run the race together.

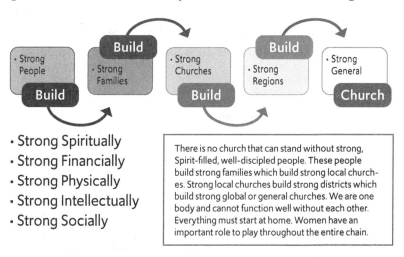

• Strong Spiritually
• Strong Financially
• Strong Physically
• Strong Intellectually
• Strong Socially

There is no church that can stand without strong, Spirit-filled, well-discipled people. These people build strong families which build strong local churches. Strong local churches build strong districts which build strong global or general churches. We are one body and cannot function well without each other. Everything must start at home. Women have an important role to play throughout the entire chain.

The role of a minister is to raise up leaders and strengthen the next generation to function well, both in our presence and in our absence. We must be intentional about this—otherwise the church will have no future. I therefore charge our women of God to build up the people who are around us. Andy Stanley said on Twitter, "Your greatest contribution to the kingdom of God may not be something you do but someone you raise."[2]

The big question for women in ministry is this: how many people have you raised in your lifetime? What legacy are you leaving behind? Your legacy will be the people whom you have raised to serve Jesus. Sure, raising money for ministry is good, and raising money for building churches is good—but the legacy of *people* will last for eternity. God, help us in our ministry to realize that the best legacy is to build people around us to a level higher than ourselves! It takes a person with a godly heart to humble themselves and raise up others. We all have egos and want to be successful, and that's not easy to give up, but we remember the example of Mary, who "treasured up all these things and pondered them in her heart" (Luke 2:19). Jesus's greatness doesn't shock Mary because she knew that her assignment was to give birth to someone, and something, greater than herself. That may be hard to swallow for some because we all want to be seen and recognized for our accomplishments.

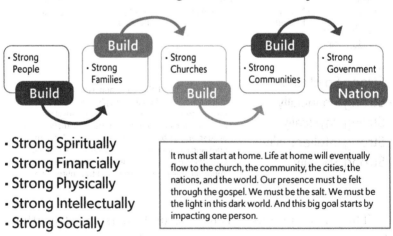

- Strong Spiritually
- Strong Financially
- Strong Physically
- Strong Intellectually
- Strong Socially

It must all start at home. Life at home will eventually flow to the church, the community, the cities, the nations, and the world. Our presence must be felt through the gospel. We must be the salt. We must be the light in this dark world. And this big goal starts by impacting one person.

---

2. Andy Stanley, on Twitter, April 17, 2013, https://twitter.com/andystanley/status/324713440541290498?lang=en.

The prophet Isaiah speaks to the generational significance of ministry: "Yes, think about Abraham, your ancestor, and Sarah, who gave birth to your nation. Abraham was only one man when I called him. But when I blessed him, he became a great nation" (Isaiah 51:2, NLT). Women who are called by God, the choice is yours. If you do not share the gospel, you do not have the love of God in you, and if you are not willing to lay down your life for the next generation, you may not actually be called. "For David, after he had served his own generation by the will of God, fell asleep, was buried with his fathers, and saw corruption" (Acts 13:36, NKJV). To minister means there cannot be a focus on self. Instead, the focus must be on becoming a blessing to the people and nations around you.

My husband and I have developed a structure for discipleship in our local church, illustrated below. Everyone in church must go through four stages of what we call the Church Cycle: Connect, Convert, Coach, Commission. When they finish, they lead someone to Christ and help them walk the same journey.

As you build your community, do so with your family. Make them part of what God is doing in your life. In this way you become one team, embracing everyone's journey of spirituality and growth. Be careful not to leave your family behind on your journey but to always work together as a team. Often I include my husband and give him room to assist me where I am weak. My husband is my best friend, my pillar of strength, and my strongest encourager. We honor God when we cherish such relationships.

Believe That God Called You

We must all have confidence in the God who called us, believing that he brought us to earth as a gift to our generation. Certain assignments have your name on them from heaven,

105

and nowhere else. Only you can do what God has planned for your life. Therefore, you have an opportunity to partner with God and, like Abraham, be a blessing to the nations. That's why your response matters to God. If you choose not to respond with a yes, then God will not force you, but he will find someone to do the work. "From the east I summon a bird of prey; from a far-off land, a man to fulfill my purpose. What I have said, that I will bring about; what I have planned, that I will do" (Isaiah 46:11). God will continue to work with or without you, and it may hurt to watch others doing what you know you should have been doing.

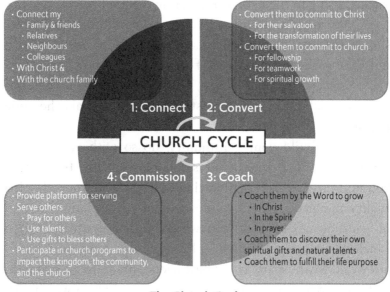

The Church Cycle

To create a nation, God used Abraham. To rescue Israel from Pharaoh, God used Moses. To defeat Jericho, God used Joshua. To save the Hebrew children, God used Esther. To preserve humanity in the flood, God used Noah. To bring back

Israel from exile, God used Daniel. In every generation, God placed and called someone, and so it is with you.

Claim the Unique Gifts God Gave You

Women are known to be multi-taskers, but sometimes that becomes a distraction to staying in your lane. It's important to know your strengths and maximize on that which you were given to transform lives around you. Never try to be something you are not. Stick to your calling and your assignment.

When God calls Moses in the burning bush and tells him to go and lead the children of Israel into the promised land, Moses is afraid and does not have faith. He keeps asking God questions. But God's response to Moses is interesting: "Then the LORD said to him, 'What is that in your hand?' 'A staff,' he replied" (Exodus 4:2). God wants Moses to identify what he already has because God will never ask us to use something we don't have or that he won't supply. God knows what is within us because he is the one who has deposited it in us. We are not a surprise to God. Our limitations or inadequacies do not surprise him. God knows and will be with us all the way to help and provide assistance. Women of God should be encouraged and be the best they can be for God.

Women in ministry need to be careful not to envy other women's gifts, talents, and strength. Recognize what God has given you, be faithful in your path, and God will bless you. Do not compete with anyone, do not compare yourself to others, and do not compromise what God has given you. Excel in who you are, even if people do not properly receive you or appreciate your work. God sees you, and he will use you for his kingdom.

My talents and gifts are few: pastor, preacher, psalmist. These are what I have in my hand right now. I use them to faithfully serve, and I trust God to do the rest. In other areas where I am not gifted, I stay away unless God wants to stretch me. In that case, I must be sure it is God and not my personal ambition. Writing to Timothy, Paul says: "For this reason, I am reminding you to fan into flames the gift of God that is within you through the laying on of my hands" (2 Timothy 1:6, ISV). Keep your gifting alive! Fan into flames the gifts God gave you!

Pray

Over and over again we read in God's Word about Jesus's prayer life. "Now in the morning, having risen a long while before daylight, he went out and departed to a solitary place; and there he prayed" (Mark 1:35, NKJV). For a successful and joyful ministry, you must develop a habit of prayer. Quiet time with God is so important. Jesus himself, the Son of God, woke up early in the morning and prayed. He was able to go to a solitary place so he could talk with the Father. It takes humility to pray, and that may become a stumbling block for some. Prayer must be prioritized and become part of our daily lives and ministry. Jesus was very much aware that his assignment on earth was huge and that there was no way he could fulfill his mission without prayer. When we pray, we get new strength on a daily basis to do the work of God.

A lack of prayer is a sign of pride, and can lead to sin. Pride makes it impossible to develop a right perspective toward God and our fellow human beings. Pride deceives (Jeremiah 49:16) and hardens the heart. When we do not pray, we are simply telling God we can handle our lives by ourselves and don't need his help. Honestly, life is difficult without God, and ministry even more so.

When we pray, we acknowledge that God is the reason for our existence in life and ministry, and that in our own strength we cannot do anything. Put God first in prayer and spend time with him in the Word and in the fellowship of the Holy Spirit. When you do your part, you will see God respond. It's easy to get busy and somehow get out in front of God. Be careful not to leave the one who has called you behind while you are representing him. The temptation is for your ministry to become all-consuming, taking all your time and energy. You must work to intentionally cultivate your relationship with Jesus Christ *first*, or else your work will be in vain.

It is my hope that these strategies, which come from my ministry in South Africa, can become valuable in any context. I have learned that all my trust and all my focus must be on God. The call I have received and the ways I live it out are to give glory to God, not to me. When the question of the call becomes more about who I am as a person rather than who God is as the one who called me, we have a problem. The answer comes for all who are called in the form of humility. May we humbly come before our heavenly Father on a daily basis, and may he always be the driving force of the work we do. May God get the glory!

Eight
Synergy in Partnership

Rev. Cara Shonamon
Co-lead Pastor
Russia and United States

The word "synergy" refers to two things that are greater together than they are apart. Synergy is what comes to mind when women and men serve together as a team in ministry. There is much joy and beauty to be found in diverse ministry teams. Does it take more effort to minister on a diverse team? Yes! Is it worth it? Yes!

As we have seen in previous chapters, women and men are created uniquely in the image of God. We have explored themes throughout church history and Scripture that point to the beauty found in both men and women serving together. Women and men are stronger when we serve together in ministry. Down to our very bones we are unique, but at the same time, God has created us to minister together. Genesis 1:27 says, "So God created mankind in his own image, in the image of God he created them; male and female he created them." This verse shows that the entire image of God is reflected when women and men are together. Verse 31 goes on to say, "God saw all that he had made, and it was very good."

All leaders and all ministers have strengths and weaknesses. Recognizing our strengths and acknowledging our weaknesses is not a limiting factor in ministry. In fact, it's liberating. When we live into the gifts and abilities that God has given us uniquely in ministry, we are able to reflect the entire image of God. When women and men express our ministry skills in ways that God has uniquely gifted us, we have the privilege to work together, humbly showing the world the love of Jesus.

Intentional Encouragement

I have learned so much from being married to my amazing husband, Justin. It is evident that each of us has our own strengths. We make each other better. For example, I have given birth to three babies and have had the joy of nursing all of them. That is something my husband cannot do! Justin is uniquely gifted to be the dad to our three children, and there are ways he can be present for them that I cannot. That is a gift. Justin and I are a team, and we are better parents when we work together.

When women and men in ministry—and in life in general—stop seeing each other as a threat but instead as a gift or an asset, as a facet of the image of God, then it is not a challenge but a joy to serve together. It is a pleasure to support one another and highlight the beautiful variety of gifts God has given all of us. Men and women can celebrate and appreciate one another.

I have had the privilege of playing on many sports teams throughout my life. I love being part of a team and watching as the gifting of many different people comes together to achieve something special. I am so glad I've never played on a team made up entirely of Caras. Sometimes I find myself distracted. I am not patient. In fact, my nickname growing up was "relentless." I loved chasing down the ball and going for the goal. There are times when that type of player is beneficial on a soccer field, but it would not be beneficial to have eleven of those players all doing the same thing at the same time! This principle applies to ministry as well. If only men serve in ministry, then a fundamental aspect of the image of God is missing. The flip side is also true: if only women served, a piece of the image of God would be missing. Men and women need each other because, when men and women work together, they get to reflect the deep love of God.

If I can be so bold, **brothers in Christ**, it's time to lose the ego. It's time to embrace humility and recognize that your sisters in Christ have much to offer in the call to ministry.

If I can be so bold, **sisters in Christ**, it's time to embrace the reality that God has called us confidently. Far too often we struggle with Imposter Syndrome, wondering if we really belong. Doubt may be an indicator that we are not trusting God's call in our lives. Will ministry be full of challenges? Absolutely. Will there be uphill battles? Absolutely. However, when we are confident in our calling, we can rest assured that God will gift us for the call. Sisters, embrace confidently the call that God has put on your life.

Brothers in Christ, you are needed to lift women up in ministry. Actions speak louder than words. We are often tempted to lean toward tokenism, but God didn't create tokens. Instead, God created women and men to be in strong partnership, united together in the mission of God. Intentional action may be needed to make space for voices that are not normally heard. Resist the temptation to be the first to speak. When you are in a meeting, practice allowing others to speak up. Let the women be first to answer. It will be a humbling experience.

If you heard an idea that you agree with and appreciate from a woman in the room, acknowledge and echo that idea while affirming the person who suggested it. Often when a woman presents an idea, it is not heard, but when a man says the same thing, people respond. Try a response something like this: "My sister in Christ said it so well, and I want to affirm what she just shared." When ideas are acknowledged, affirmed, and echoed, they gain traction. Women will continue to offer their voices and their ideas when they are shown that their input is appreciated.

Sisters in Christ, we belong! Therefore, we need to act like it. That does not mean we become like men or that we need to lead like men to fit in. It does mean we need to be comfortable in our own skin. Do not apologize for who you are. We do not need to apologize for being mothers *or* for not being mothers. We do not need to apologize for showing emotions. God equips those whom God calls, and when God calls women to ministry, that calling indicates a unique and necessary set of gifts.

Models of Partnership

I have seen numerous examples of the beauty of women and men serving in ministry together. My Grandma and Grandpa Sunberg served together in ministry. Grandpa was a pastor, and Grandma supported his ministry. The fact that so many of the Sunberg kids and grandkids serve the Lord faithfully as ministers or laity in the church is a testament to the partnership—the synergy of ministry—that took place in Bill and Thelma Sunberg's house. Bill and Thelma lived out their faith in local church ministry. Sometimes they served in difficult places, yet they learned to leave places of ministry better than they found them.

I've heard my father share about a particularly difficult moment in ministry for my grandparents. My grandfather was voted out of the church after a few disgruntled individuals rounded up all the voting members they could find. They had to pack up their belongings and move out of the parsonage. As they left, one of the board members who had given them a hard time came over to see if they had wrecked the parsonage. The thought of leaving the parsonage in poor condition had never crossed Bill or Thelma's mind. They left the house in better shape than they'd found it. My grandfather greeted the man, shook his hand, and said goodbye without anger or malice. This was the beauty of the synergy between Bill and Thelma Sunberg. They lived out their faith in front of their children. They honored each other. They respected each other, they shared their faith together, and their children have pointed to that moment as building their faith as they saw their parents, together, reflect Christ.

My Grandma and Grandpa Johnson also lived out their faith together in ministry. My grandmother received her college degree in Christian education. My grandfather received his college degree in pastoral ministry. They went into ministry together right out of college. Following several pastorates in the Pacific Northwest, they moved to Germany to serve the church as missionaries. In Germany, my grandfather served as a pastor and a missionary, and my grandmother served as a missionary and was one of the first professors at the European Nazarene Bible College. My mother tells stories of how Grandma Alice and Grandpa Jerry poured into the lives of those in the community. It was evident that Alice and Jerry lived a synergistic life, serving God together in ministry.

Years later, when they moved to Kansas City, Alice became a children's pastor, and Jerry served as the director of World Mission for the Church of the Nazarene. They were always looking for ways to serve the Lord. In the last phase of their lives, they lived in a retirement community in Meridian, Idaho. Every Sunday afternoon, they helped lead a service for the residents in their community. They did not know how to stop serving. They continued to serve the Lord together until Grandma Alice passed away, followed by Grandpa Jerry a year later. They are rejoicing in the presence of Jesus today.

I have also seen the beauty of the synergy of women and men in ministry lived out in the lives of my parents. My parents moved us to Moscow, Russia, in 1992, where we served as missionaries for the next thirteen years. My parents were intentional to include my older sister, Christy, and me in the life and ministry of the church. Christy and I were convinced that we were missionaries as well. We even were a little put off when our names didn't appear in a publication that listed the birthdays of various missionaries around the globe. Our parents told us we *were* missionaries and that God had called us too.

My mother received her undergraduate degree in nursing, and my father received his in pastoral ministry. When we lived in Russia, my mom used a lot of her nursing knowledge to lead medical mission teams and various other compassionate ministry initiatives. After a few years of living in Russia, something stirred within my mom that she had been wrestling with for quite some time. It was her call. My sister and I saw my dad support her discernment of the call. When I was in middle school and my sister was in high school, our mother traveled to the United States for two weeks at a time, twice a year, to work on her master's degree.

I find myself blessed to see the synergy of women and men in ministry lived out in front of me by my own parents. They continue to support each other in ministry today. There have been lots of stops along the way, but now my father and I serve together as co-lead pastors of a local church, and my mom serves as a general superintendent in the Church of the Nazarene. They love and support each other in their unique calls to ministry, but they also see that they are called together in ministry.

I am thankful for the example of my grandparents and my parents and their calls to ministry. I am forever indebted to them. Because of their witness and their example, I never thought twice about my own call.

Special Gifts

My journey into ministry has been unique. I grew up on the mission field, and my dad tells a story about how one day I ran into the room and said, "Hey, Dad! Who is going to carry on the family business?" This was my way of saying, "Who is going to be a pastor next?" I recognized there was a pattern in our family of people becoming pastors.

My dad's response was, "I don't know, maybe you?"

Fast forward a few years, and we moved to the United States between my sophomore and junior year of high school. I played on the soccer team at my high school, and as a result, I was able to play soccer at Olivet Nazarene University as well. On the soccer team at Olivet, I enjoyed playing my guitar before games, leading the team in worship. One day I met with my coach, and he asked if I had ever considered getting a local minister's license. I had not. I was majoring in history and political science, but I felt so challenged that I called my dad later that day and asked him what he thought about me pursuing my local license. I remember him saying he was proud of me—more proud than he'd been at any of my soccer games. This was a big deal because, at that time, sports ran my life. I went home for Christmas that year and was given the opportunity to preach.

Dr. Dean, my history professor at Olivet, was also a great mentor for me. He and his wife pastored a small rural church together. After he learned of my call to preach, he offered me the opportunity to preach at his church while he and his wife went on a two-week vacation. As a junior in college this was an incredible gift—that my professor believed and trusted in me. My husband and I met and got engaged in college. We began to think about our future together and decided to drive to Kansas City to explore the idea of me attending Nazarene Theological Seminary, and for him to look for teaching opportunities. As we left the seminary's parking lot after our visit, my husband said to me, "You belong here." What a gift!

Transitions and New Paradigms

While I attended seminary, I had the joy of serving two local churches in the Kansas City area as children's pastor, and I loved every minute. I was then called to serve as a children's pastor at a church in Flint, Michigan. Justin and I loved our time in Flint, where we formed many lasting relationships. We even bought twelve acres of land with a house and started a small farm. We were deeply invested in the people and the area. Flint will forever hold a special place in my heart. It is where Justin and I welcomed both of our daughters into our lives.

While we were in Flint, a nudging began in both our hearts. We began to sense it was time to make a change. We did not know what that meant, but I knew I was not called to be a children's pastor forever. I loved serving as a children's pastor and did not think of this ministry as a stepping-stone to something else. I simply knew God had called me to preach and lead a church. Justin and I began to prayerfully seek what God had in store for us. At the same time, my father had been serving as interim pastor at one of the churches where I had served as children's pastor while I was in seminary. The church asked my dad to become their full-time lead pastor. His response was that he was called to join his wife in ministry, so he did not feel it was right for him to commit to a full-time pastorate, but he told them he would be open to serving part-time. The church prayerfully considered their options and ended up hiring my dad and me to serve together as co-lead pastors.

It has been an absolute joy to serve as co-lead pastor with my dad. It takes some effort for this unique relationship to work, but I have watched as my dad has put his ego aside and encouraged the women in his life to shine for Jesus. My father always told my sister and me that, with God's help, we could change the world. My sister serves in England writing policy to help end homelessness. She is changing the world with God's help. I am called to ministry, and I desire to serve in any way that God will use me.

Practically speaking, it is beautiful to be on a team where both men and women are serving together. There are instances where Chuck (my father) connects better with a parishioner, and other times when I am more easily able to develop a relationship. It does not necessarily have to do with gender. Also, there is a beauty to serving together intergenerationally. Chuck brings a unique perspective from many years in ministry and, because of that, is able to connect to many of our parishioners. I bring a unique view with fresh eyes and lots of ideas. When the two perspectives come together, a sharpening happens between us. I seek Chuck's advice on how things have been done in the past, and he is curious about where God is leading younger generations. So, as we work together, we put our egos aside and seek God first. Prayer becomes central for both of us as we desire for God to be first in all we say and do. On our staff, we have a fantastic group of women and men serving together in ministry. It is beautiful. We make one another better. We think differently. We have different strengths. We encourage one another in different ways. I would not have it any other way. We truly are better together.

A friend once told me that I had a degree from Making Stuff Up University. Do you have a degree from there as well?

Sometimes as women in ministry, we are good at making stuff up. We create a negative narrative in our minds and then begin to live into the story we have created. Sisters in Christ, we need to submit those thoughts and insecurities to God. When we daily submit those thoughts to God, we are able to lay aside the fabricated narrative that often renders us lame and ineffective. When we embrace all that God has for us and embrace God's narrative, we can change the world.

There will absolutely be people who will not support a woman called to ministry, but we must remember it is God's call. Therefore, our accountability is before God. We must be faithful in prayer and patient in affliction. If anyone is frustrated with a woman in ministry, the response must be made in a spirit of love—for people remember how they are treated.

Brothers and sisters in Christ, we are better together, and we need each other. Brothers in Christ, I am thankful for you. I am thankful we get to be part of the kingdom of God together. Sisters in Christ, I am thankful for you. I am thankful we get to be part of the kingdom of God together. May we join together and share the great love of Jesus while serving in tandem, not an opposition. When we do so, we will shine the amazing light of Jesus in this dark and weary world.

Nine
Walking through a Crisis in Ministry

Rev. Dr. Tammy Carter
Lead Pastor
Director, International Board of Education for the Global Church
United States

The storm begins as a small cluster of clouds off the coast of a continent half a world away. Often, the gathering clouds go unnoticed as they build, moving across the planet, gathering energy and strength from the ocean below. By the time this small series of storms reaches the coast near you, it has developed into a full-blown, Category 5 hurricane that has the attention of the world. By the time the storm impacts your life, all you are left to do is respond to the damage left in its wake. Crisis in ministry is very much like a hurricane, in that there is a starting point. Often the crisis begins as something small, like a health concern or moral compromise. Sometimes it hits hard and fast, like a pandemic that shuts down economies and routines overnight. Either way, there are real implications and valuable lessons we can learn from walking through a crisis while in ministry.

This chapter is written from personal experience and conversations with many women in ministry who have gone through extreme crisis caused by shocking health news, spiritual lapse—either their own or their partner's—financial crisis, or another type of crisis. In some cases, we admit that the crisis is of our own making, but in many cases we are thrown into crisis suddenly and without warning by the actions and decisions of someone else. We discover there are some lessons to learn about negotiating through the unique realities of dealing with a crisis while in ministry.

In many places, women in leadership are already in a precarious position. A crisis could give the church reason to pull away from her and question her ability to lead. It would be shortsighted to presume that, just because she is facing a crisis, her leadership has failed. It is exactly during a time of crisis when a woman in leadership needs church leaders to support her and allow the necessary time for processing and healing. In my experience, the steady prayer and verbal support of others in leadership strengthened me. Beyond their presence with me, I am aware there were times when key leaders took up a position of protection around me. They decided to protect me while I remained in my position of leadership, while I walked through dark valleys caused by crisis. In fact, not only did they not sideline me, but they also called me to step into new roles. It occurred to me at the time that, if we are going to have women in leadership, not only do we need to open doors, but we also need to protect and support them even as they face challenges, crisis, and especially the blessing of welcoming children into their family lives. The voice of our women in leadership is vital to the health and well-being of the global church. As leaders—both lay and clergy—we need to support women and protect them as they lead us forward. We will receive the blessings of the lessons they learn from their journey through crisis while in leadership.

Guilt and shame quickly bubble to the top of anyone's emotions when we are in crisis. In the initial response, it is common to blame oneself, even if the cause was completely outside our responsibility. In our attempt to explain what happened, the easiest person to blame is the self. Throughout Scripture we see examples of this when questions are asked almost every time something goes wrong. Someone is sick: what is their sin? A catastrophic event occurs: what or whose sin caused it? The questions, the blame, the guilt, and the shame come naturally as we try to figure out the cause of the events that leave us broken and desperate. Crisis gives rise to both shame (the overwhelming sense that I am inadequate and broken) and guilt (the realization that I have done something wrong). The women I spoke to agreed that it didn't matter if the crisis was demonstrably their fault—they had a strong sense of both shame and guilt either way.

Dealing with guilt requires us to look honestly into a situation and evaluate our role in it. We must own our responsibility, repent before God, apologize, and make amends to those impacted by our actions. Receiving God's forgiveness and grace and being in right relationship with others releases us from guilt.

Shame can be harder—because we are hard on ourselves, and we live in cultures where shame is a powerful motivator and manipulator. If you are filled with shame, it is important to take time to understand the source so you can separate yourself from it and allow yourself to see and confess that this crisis is not your fault. You must speak truth to yourself if you are going to get a correct perspective on the shame and guilt that seem to continually dance in your head.

Connected to shame and guilt is also failure. As with the first two, sometimes it is our fault. We failed, and that failure spun into a larger crisis. When failure and guilt are appropriate, our response needs to be confession and a commitment to change the way we live and lead.

We live in a society, especially within the church, where everything is measured. It is easy to get caught in the trap of believing that, because the numbers don't line up, we are a failure. During crisis it is especially hard to make the numbers add up. Often, numbers take a deep dive during crisis, and we are challenged to deal with our sense of failure when we don't measure up to someone else's expectations.

Recently, someone close to me created a crisis situation that touched every corner of my life and ministry. I was overwhelmed with the sense of failure. Nothing would be the same again. My world had collapsed. While I repeated a mantra of failure, a dear friend and church leader said to me, "Leadership is not about never failing. Leadership is about what happens after you fail." That statement was life-transforming for me. Suddenly it didn't matter how far I had fallen, how deeply I'd been buried, or even how much of the responsibility I personally bore. It was about what happened next. Before was less important than next. This failure would not define me, or how I responded to it, but how I withstood the storm would be a testimony to my identity as a leader and to the identity of the God at work in my life. What happens after failure isn't about you. It is about how you allow God to work in your life to transform and renew you as a living testimony of the almighty God.

In all the conversations about crisis in ministry, regardless of circumstance, grief was a significant player in the process. There is the grieving of what was lost, including what now can never be. There is the grieving of lost relationships, lost status, shaken stability, and loss of hope. As joy and clarity are replaced with depression and uncertainty, there is loss of self, which becomes one of the most difficult things to grieve. The stages of grief are not linear. Journeying through grief is like hiking in the mountains. At points the hike is easy and manageable. Then there are rocks to climb over, streams to cross, and perhaps occasionally a perilous rope bridge to navigate. Sometimes the hike is uphill, and then the path takes a turn, and in order to reach the next summit you must go downhill again. There are twists and turns in the path, and often you will not be able to see where it leads. Navigating grief requires great courage to continue putting one foot in front of the other along the path, trusting that this is the path toward healing and restoration.

What I repeatedly heard from the women in these conversations was that grief is one of the most difficult realities of crisis to manage. Grief is sneaky. Just when you think you are past it and moving forward again, a memory is tickled, and grief comes rushing back in to overwhelm you. Culturally, many of us are not allowed enough time to grieve. Caring people around us press in on us to "get over it" and "move on." Of course, their concern is that we will get stuck. The problem is that, by moving on too quickly, we short-circuit the deep, hard, meaningful work that good grieving requires. We must find ways to give ourselves permission to grieve, not for the sake of self-pity or self-loathing but to reach the point of finding the meaning behind what is causing the grief. When we sit with our grief long enough to learn from it, we will be able to move forward in health and strength.

One of the ways to begin moving forward is to practice gratitude. It is amazing how the simple activity of expressing gratitude can change your perspective, breathe hope into your life, and begin to clear a path to move forward with a clearer vision of the future. Being grateful begins as an act of discipline. At first, it will be difficult because grief and hopelessness are overwhelming. However, the more your words and actions express thanksgiving to God and others, the more you will be transformed into a grateful person.

Gratitude also begins to transform prayer. Before we are able to be grateful, our prayers are often driven by needy requests, lament, and desperate cries for help. As we practice gratitude, our perspective begins to shift, and we are able to see a bigger picture. With good discipline, your prayer life will be transformed from screaming and begging to listening and learning. Prayer isn't about declaring our laundry list. Prayer is learning to be in the presence of the almighty God.

Pray until you are able to move beyond the lists and pleas. Pray until you are all prayed out and all that is left is being with God. Pray without ceasing with every breath you breathe. Pray, even if all you can do is give thanks to God for the breath you have to breathe. Sit, stand, kneel, lie down, walk, run, drive—try different positions and places. Read prayers from Scripture or from those who have walked in darkness before you. Don't make it complicated. Prayer is simply communication with God. Sometimes the most powerful communication in a loving relationship is the willingness to simply sit and be still with the other.

The power of learning to be present, especially during times of crisis, is a skill that requires discipline and intentionality. Also, like prayer and gratitude, being present requires practice. Barbara Brown Taylor talks about the gift of darkness in her book *Learning to Walk in the Dark*. As children, we are taught to come in out of the darkness, but Taylor argues there is much to learn by sitting in darkness long enough to begin seeing, to begin noticing what God is trying to teach us, to begin learning from the darkness and being inspired to live in the light.[1]

In his book, *Dare: The New Way to End Anxiety and Stop Panic Attacks*, Barry McDonagh writes that we need to learn to accept the anxiety and get comfortable with it. He creates an almost humorous image of inviting our anxiety in to sit with us in friendly curiosity. Can you imagine yourself serving tea to your depression, fear, grief? Welcome it. Embrace it. Sit and learn from it as if it is an elderly friend who has great wisdom to dispatch to you.[2]

For most of us, avoiding pain is a more natural response than embracing it. Yet, as both these authors remind us, it is in the dark, hard places of life that we learn our greatest lessons, including our total dependence on God. As we learn in the darkness, we begin a metamorphic transformation like a butterfly inside a dark cocoon. Crisis changes us. Gold is purified by fire, and diamonds are created under tremendous pressure. We are neither diamonds nor gold, but finding ourselves in the middle of crisis can create an opportunity to see ourselves in a new light that causes us to confess our need for God, and God's transformative power. In our brokenness, we become aware of our need for God to restore us. We are worthy of God's work in our lives because we are made in the image of God. In Christ, we are worthy of God's restorative work.

The Hebrew understanding of restoration has at its core the idea of restoring someone or something to a state that is even better than the original. The Japanese have an art form called *kintsukuroi* ("golden repair") or *kintsugi* ("golden joinery"). It is a process of repairing pottery with gold or silver lacquer so the

---

1. Barbara Brown Taylor, *Learning to Walk in the Dark* (San Francisco: HarperOne, 2014).

2. Barry McDonagh, *Dare: The New Way to End Anxiety and Stop Panic Attacks* (Ireland: BMD Publishing Ltd., 2015).

final piece is more beautiful than the original. When you find your life broken in the middle of an impossible crisis situation, it may be hard to imagine that God loves you and will restore you. It may be impossible to see the hope of another day. It may be impossible to see beyond the darkness, beyond the deep hole you find yourself in, or beyond the moment. However, God has not forgotten you. God has not abandoned you. God has not turned away from you. On the contrary, God is closer and more accessible than ever. Don't allow your emotions to drive your thinking during this time. Reach deep into your faith and spiritual disciplines to allow God access to the most broken parts of your life. Draw close to God and allow the transformation to move across your life and ministry.

The final step in learning to thrive in and through crisis in ministry is to discern the meaning from the experience and be able to teach what you have learned. Much that happens during a crisis will be left behind, but what are the key lessons you should carry forward from this place into the next season of your life? What have you learned that can guide you in the future? What is the meaning you can exegete from your life in crisis that you can teach to others?

Remember, crisis does not define you. *Whose* you are defines *who* you are. Being created in the image of God defines you. The decision to learn from and through crisis, to allow yourself to be broken and restored by the Master's touch, to decide to breathe until you can move on and lead from the crisis is what will carry you forward. God in you will define who you are. Be careful not to allow the crises of your life to define who you are. Allow crisis to be a journey of learning, growing, and transforming. Allow crisis to wake you up spiritually so you can become a stronger leader. The butterfly is not defined by the darkness of the cocoon. Yet, without the cocoon, the caterpillar can never become the beautiful butterfly. Without the cocoon, the caterpillar never has the opportunity to soar through the air or lead a migration across continents. The cocoon doesn't define the butterfly. *After* the butterfly twists and turns and fights its way free of the cocoon, its beauty breaks forth, and the world understands it is a butterfly.

You are loved and fearfully and wonderfully made in the image of the one true God. Your worth is in your relationship to God—not in your job, talents, possessions, relationships, or anything else you can name. What happens in a moment of crisis is only part of your story. Be strong and courageous. Learn, grow, heal, and be restored so that—as you twist and turn and fight your way free of the crises that bear down on you—you too will be able to launch forward with new meaning and messages of hope and grace for a world caught in its own crises. As you soar into the future, you will lead a generation into life-transforming relationships with God.

Ten
Becoming a Champion

Rev. Dr. David Downs
District Superintendent
United States

I have to admit that it's getting better—though there are still some big challenges out there. Take, for example, the outspoken male parishioner who met Pastor Karen at the platform on her first Sunday as interim pastor of a small church near the Ohio River.

"You need to know that I don't believe in women preachers!" he declared.

"Well," she gently replied, "you'll have to take that up with the Lord. He's the one who called me to preach."

I, as district superintendent, had asked the congregation to consider Karen as a pastoral candidate. She was a seasoned veteran with a good record, and gifted in many ways that specifically matched the needs of this hurting congregation. Karen had led numerous people to the Lord over the years. Her spouse was supportive, meaning she could afford to accept a part-time pastoral salary. Furthermore (foremost, actually), I had sensed the Lord's direction in this pastoral assignment. I thought the congregation would be delighted.

I was surprised and, frankly, perturbed when the secretary of the church board—a godly woman in whom I had much confidence—called to report the board's decision not to even interview Karen. "We have a man in our church who doesn't believe in women ministers. We don't want to hurt his feelings. He's stated that he and his family will leave the church if we call Karen as our pastor."

"Well, I have an idea," I replied. "Let's ask her to serve as interim and see what the Lord can do."

And, just as I thought would be the case, the congregation loved Pastor Karen. At the close of her first sermon, the altars were filled with seekers. It was apparent to all that Karen's ministry was anointed and that God's call was on her life. At the center of the altar, crying tears of repentance, was the man who didn't believe in women preachers. This time, he met Karen at the steps leading off the platform to apologize.

The board secretary called that afternoon to report that the board met immediately after the service and wanted to call Karen as their permanent pastor. She accepted and had a fruitful ministry there until her retirement. The man who challenged her call became an ardent supporter and later joined both the church and the board.

When it comes to women in ministry in the Church of the Nazarene, things *are* getting better! For one thing, a biblical theology of women in ministry has been integrated into the prescribed course of study for Nazarene pastors. Over the years, we've learned that the recounting of our heritage of female clergy from the early days of our denomination, as powerful and beautiful as that heritage is, is not a sufficient argument against those—whether from other traditions or our own—who see female clergy as anathema.

It is important that we continue to tell our story, which is filled with powerful examples of courageous female founding pastors. On the district I oversee in Texas, which covers a large segment from the western half of the Dallas/Fort Worth metropolis through the western cities of Amarillo and Lubbock, we frequently recount the stories of women who stepped up a century ago and planted numerous congregations. We celebrate women like Mary Lee Cagle, who founded many of the congregations that are *still* leading churches on the district. Those of us who've been in the Church of the Nazarene for a while have been deeply enriched by the legacy of these courageous women. However, when it comes time for a church board to actually extend a call to a woman to serve as their pastor, I've learned that relying on our heritage for persuasion is not usually enough.

As a district superintendent, I've learned that those in our churches who oppose women ministers often mean well but are misinformed. There is strong biblical evidence to support women in clergy roles, as previous chapters in this book have shown. Our leaders need to be aware of this evidence so that, for instance, board members who have been taught over the years that women should not be in the pulpit can be shown the biblical record.

When I went through the Nazarene education and clergy preparation system as a student, the subject of female clergy was almost never discussed. There were occasional mentions of great women in our history, but there was little to no discussion of the biblical teaching regarding the validity of a woman's call to ministry. Fortunately, this is changing. It began changing for me in 2004, when missionary Michael Park was serving in Central Asia. He was one of my former students from when I'd served as a missionary and professor at Korea Nazarene Theological College in the '90s. He asked me to bring a group of pastors and professors to Kazakhstan, where he was the pioneer missionary for our denomination. In just a few short years, the church had blossomed. Michael was responsible for twenty or so new congregations and had a wonderful group of prospective young pastors—half of whom were women. They were filled with the joy and enthusiasm of young believers. They were excited about what God had done in their lives, and they were confident regarding what the Lord could do in their new country, which had recently become independent from the Soviet Union.

However, upon meeting these precious students, we were particularly concerned about the future ministries of the women. Up to that point, no one had ever challenged the validity of their call. We knew that someday, as Christianity grew in Kazakhstan, someone would. I asked one of our pastors, Tracy Ogden Johnson, if she could teach a crash biblical theology course on women in ministry. She agreed, and the class was amazing. The Kazakh students accepted it as somewhat matter of fact, but for many others, including myself, it was a great *aha!* moment. I don't know how many theology degrees we had among us (I had four), but this was a new and fresh perspective for most, if not all, of us.

When we returned home, I asked Pastor Ogden-Johnson to teach this class on our district, first to all the pastors, and then to each of the district-licensed ministers coming up through the Course of Study. Soon, our ministerial studies board made Tracy's course mandatory for district licensure and ordination. I wish all of our pastors (and particularly our leaders), denomination-wide, could take her course.

Several years after this experience in Kazakhstan, I was on the floor of the 2012 Nazarene General Assembly when a distinguished-looking woman tapped my shoulder and introduced herself. "I am Pastor Zhanna. I remember you from your visits to Kazakhstan," she said. When I asked her to tell me about her current assignment, she replied, "I am now the district superintendent of the church in Kazakhstan."

Yes, things are getting better. The USA/Canada Regional Course of Study Advisory Committee (RCOSAC) has prioritized the integration of Biblical Theology of Women in Ministry into its approved curriculum for ministerial preparation. Recent data supports the growing status of Nazarene women clergy. According to Nazarene research specialist Richard Houseal, the percentage of women in pastoral positions in the Church of the Nazarene grew from 1908 through 1935. In a paper Houseal presented in 2003 to the Association of Nazarene Sociologists and Researchers, however, he reported the following: "Their [women's] percentage of total pastoral positions peaked back in 1925. From 1925–1935, the number of women in pastoral roles, though increasing, did not keep pace with the number of men. After 1935 and continuing through 1950, there were small declines in the number of female pastors; however, these small declines accelerated the percentage declines because the number of male pastors continued to increase."[1]

Houseal points out that the number of women in pastoral ministry peaked in 1955, then began to shrink rapidly. He laments, "The gains for women in pastoral positions were short-lived, and again declined every year in both number and percent until 1985."[2] By 1985, the percentage of women Nazarene pastors in the U.S. had fallen from a high of 12.2% in 1925 to an all-time low of 1.1%.[3] The good news is that, over the past two decades, the denominational data relating to the USA/Canada region is encouraging. Since 1999, the percentage

---

1. Richard Houseal, "Nazarene Clergy Women: A Statistical Analysis from 1908 to 2003," presented at the Association of Nazarene Sociologists and Researchers (ANSR) Annual Conference (2003), 4.

2. Houseal, "Nazarene Clergy Women," 5.

3. Houseal, "Nazarene Clergy Women," 10.

of women lead pastors has grown from 2.9% to 11.6%. The percentage of newly ordained women has grown during that twenty-year period from 16.3% to 35.1%. The percentage of total women clergy in our denomination has grown from 8.5% to 23.5%.[4]

While things are getting better, there is still a lot of room for improvement. Recently I met with a group of young women who serve as pastors on our district. They are of a new generation, mostly in their thirties and early forties, but each had stories to tell about the obstacles they have had to navigate as they have come into ministry. In fact, I don't think I've ever spoken to a woman pastor who cannot recount multiple experiences of gender-based discrimination. Most will not volunteer their stories because they do not wish to indict their pastors, fathers, brothers, or the church as a whole for overtly (and sometimes covertly) discouraging their divine call. Nevertheless, most have experienced the pain of invalidation and rejection. Dear Lord, please forgive us.

One of our ministers, who co-pastors one of our strongest churches alongside her husband, recounted that she often heard doubts vocalized by detractors. "I don't know if I want to have a woman lead pastor," she recalls hearing contemporaries say. As was the case a generation earlier, there was little to no affirmation of her call to ministry in college. Furthermore, a female pastorate had never been modeled for her. I have a hunch. I admit, I don't know how to prove this, but it is a strong hunch that some male clergy oppose women in ministry solely because they view the pastorate as a bastion of masculinity. They oppose women not for theological reasons but based purely on

4. Research Services, "Women Clergy Stats 1999–2019" (Lenexa, KS: Global Ministry Center for the Church of the Nazarene, 2020).

136

their own bias and, maybe, insecurity. This type of opposition is blatant sexism.

For several decades, I've been an avid motorcycle enthusiast. Specifically, I love Harley Davidsons, and I've ridden hundreds of thousands of miles through the contiguous United States. For a number of years, I was the chaplain of our local Harley Owners Group (H.O.G.). About twenty years ago, we noticed a sharp increase in the number of women riders joining our local H.O.G. chapter. I am ashamed to confess that, at first, it made me uncomfortable and perhaps even a bit insecure because I had always thought of riding these big bikes as a purely masculine experience that was shared by bearded, black-leather-wearing, tattooed, *manly* men. Soon, however, we all welcomed our new female H.O.G. members, and they quickly began to enrich the group experience. No matter how I may have tried to justify it at the time, I was guilty of blatant sexism.

Isn't the analogy to the church obvious? How many precious girls, young women, and even mature women have had their divine call thwarted due to the insecurity of their male pastors? How much damage has been done by male pastors who have failed to affirm and encourage—and, in some cases, who have actively discouraged—girls and women who have been called by Jesus to enter the ministry, not for any particular theological reason but simply due to insecurity and the bias and discrimination such insecurity leads to?

A pastor recently shared with me a tragic story about one of the leading women (the board secretary) in his church. Over the years, I'd worked with her on various projects and had come to admire her greatly. Her son became an amazing pastor, as did her daughter-in-law. I expressed to her pastor how much I appreciated this woman, who had led the congregation through a difficult interim between pastors.

"Yes," he said, "Did you know that she was called to the ministry as a young girl but never, ever received affirmation of her call or her obvious giftedness?"

She went on to be an outstanding layperson—one of the best I know—but what if she had known pastors, Sunday school teachers, parents, professors, and others who had been sensitive to the Spirit's leading in her life?

I called her, and we spoke about it. Part of the problem was that female ministerial leadership in the church had only been modeled for her once or twice when she was young. She remembers the profound experience of sitting under the preaching of a woman evangelist as a child—but even that had been minimized by some in the church.

Our leaders have a solemn responsibility to allow the body of Christ—especially young people, and particularly girls and young women—to witness strong women fulfilling ministerial and leadership roles in the church. I'm increasingly grateful for the historic leadership of all of our denomination's general superintendents, but I was especially thankful when Dr. Nina Gunter and Dr. Carla Sunberg led our district assemblies. I'm grateful for all of our camp speakers, but I've been particularly thankful when a woman such as Dr. Susie Shellenberger is our camp evangelist. I enjoy visiting all the churches on our district, but I am particularly blessed when I get to visit churches led by capable, gifted women. It is *vital* that strong, Spirit-filled, female pastoral/ministerial leadership is modeled in the church. It is vital for our future. Many of the clergywomen I know cite female role models as a major factor in their decision or ability to be faithful to the call of God on their lives.

Let's take it a step further. In addition to affirmation and modeling, Nazarene female clergy also need champions. Women can be champions, of course, but those with whom I've spoken have expressed special appreciation for men who are intentional about providing support for clergywomen. Supportive husbands are frequently cited by women ministers as their greatest champions. Other men who are often mentioned and appreciated as champions are fathers, professors, pastors, strong laymen in their congregations, and (I'm pleased to say) district superintendents. It's my belief that women of any profession would appreciate support from these men, but particularly in a profession such as ministry, where women are a distinct minority, male champions are priceless.

One pastor on my district recalls her grandfather reaching out to the religion department at her Nazarene university and expressing his concern when he learned she was changing her major from religion to psychology due to her sense of a lack of support for her call. Good for Grandfather! I would like to challenge all men to step up as champions of the girls and women in our churches whom God has called into ministry. First, of course, we must choose to change course (repent) regarding any prejudicial actions or attitudes we've harbored against women ministers. Then we must look for positive actions we can take to champion their cause—which is really God's cause.

Here are some straightforward suggestions for ways we can be champions.

In the local congregation:
- Model women in ministry by looking for every opportunity to feature women in worship leadership. When possible, welcome women to serve not only as preachers but also as Scripture readers, music leaders, and Communion assistants. Hire them as associate pastors or for other staff ministry roles that often go to men.
- Make use of every opportunity to celebrate women in leadership. Make sure local and district ministers' licenses are celebrated.

- Schedule and lead special seminars and studies regarding a biblical theology of women in ministry. Midweek services or weekend workshops would be perfect. Pastors, if you have never studied a biblical theology of women in ministry, do so as soon as possible.
- Preach a sermon series about leading women in the Bible (the chapters of this book will help you pinpoint some excellent names if you need a place to start).
- Look for every opportunity to affirm and encourage girls and women who hear a divine call.
- Be intentional *never* to discourage a ministerial calling in the life of a girl or woman who demonstrates the gifts and graces necessary for ministry. Be mindful of the fact that your spoken words have great impact.
- Make sure women are included on the church board and in other volunteer and paid leadership positions.
- In times of pastoral transition, be careful not to discriminate (and encourage your church board not to discriminate) against female candidates.

At the district level:
- Use gender-inclusive language. This is important in district publications and especially in presentations of the district superintendent when meeting with boards during pastoral transition. Be prepared to see some rolling eyes when you refer to the future pastor as "he or she" in your early meetings with a church board in pastoral transition, but your intentionality in this regard is important. Continue it throughout the process.
- Carefully consider *all* female pastoral candidates.
- Make sure district officers, beginning with the superintendent, have had meaningful training regarding a biblical theology of women in ministry.

- District superintendents should consider taking advantage of local interim opportunities, while a church is in pastoral transition, to supply the pulpit with women clergy. Interim pastoral service often leads to appointment, election, or at least serious consideration of women for pastoral positions.

- Place women in visible leadership positions at the district level. This is important on the District Advisory Board and of particular importance when it comes to credentialing boards. In recent years our district has had up to 40 percent of our district license and ordination applicants be women, yet, for many years, we had only a small percentage of women elected to the Ministerial Credentials Board. So, with our general superintendent's approval, and by a unanimous vote of our District Assembly, we added four additional women as ex-officio members, which gave us enough women to ensure that all candidates had at least one woman on their credentials interview committee.

- Whenever possible, invite women to be retreat, camp meeting, and workshop speakers.

I'm sure, even as you've read these simple suggestions for championing women in ministry, you've thought of several other ideas. As you have read the chapters of this book, I know you have undoubtedly had many ideas. Apply them, and enjoy the blessing of championing a concept that is close to the heart of God.